THE ROVER

THE ROVER

or

The Banished Cavaliers

Aphra Behn

edited by Anne Russell

second edition

broadview editions

Canada Cataloguing in Publication Data
Behn, Aphra, 1640–1689
    The Rover, or, The banished cavaliers

(Broadview literary texts)
A play.

Includes bibliographical references.
ISBN 1-55111-214-0

I. Russell, Anne Elizabeth, 1952– . II. Title.   III. Title: The banished cavaliers
IV. Series.

PR3317.R58 1998   822'.4   C98-931716-1

Broadview Press Ltd. is an independent, international publishing house, incorporated in 1985.

North America
PO Box 1243, Peterborough, Ontario, Canada K9J 7H5
Tel: (705) 743-8990; Fax: (705) 743-8353
email: customerservice@broadviewpress.com
3576 California Road, Orchard Park, NY, USA 14127

UK, Ireland, and continental Europe
NBN Plymbridge
Estover Road
Plymouth PL6 7PY UK
Tel: 44 (0) 1752 202 301
Fax: 44 (0) 1752 202 331
Fax Order Line: 44 (0) 1752 202 333
Customer Service: cservs@nbnplymbridge.com
Orders: orders@nbnplymbridge.com

Australia and New Zealand
UNIREPS, University of New South Wales
Sydney, NSW, 2052
Tel: 61 2 9664 0999; Fax: 61 2 9664 5420
email: info.press@unsw.edu.au

www.broadviewpress.com

Broadview Press is grateful to Professor Eugene Benson for advice on editorial matters for the Broadview Literary Texts Series.

Broadview Press gratefully acknowledges the financial support of the Government of Canada through the Book Publishing Industry Development Program for our publishing activities.

PRINTED IN CANADA

Contents

Acknowledgements   7

Note to the Second Edition   8

Introduction

    Aphra Behn's Life and Career   9

    Sources of *The Rover*   20

    The Rover: Critical Issues   23

    Stage History   31

    Notes   37

    Selected Bibliography   43

    A Note on the Text   51

THE ROVER

    Prologue   55

    The Actors' Names   57

    Act I   59

    Act II   82

    Act III   102

    Act IV   129

    Act V   161

    Epilogue   187

    Post-Script   189

Textual Notes   191

Appendix A: Behn on her Work

    1. From the "Epistle Dedicatory" to the *Second Part of
The Rover*   197

    2. From "A Pastoral to Mr. Stafford..."   198

Appendix B: From Early Accounts of Behn's Life
  1. From *Female Poems on Several Occasions. Written by Ephelia* 200
  2. From Gerard Langbainè *An Account of the English Dramatick Poets* 201
  3. From "The History of the Life and Memoirs of Mrs. Behn" 203
  4. From *The Poetical Register* 207
  5. From *A General Dictionary, Historical and Critical* 209

Appendix C: Adaptation
  Excerpt from J.P. Kemble's adaptation of *The Rover, Love in Many Masks...* 214

Acknowledgements

It is a pleasure to acknowledge the assistance of the many people and organizations I have been helped by in the preparation of this edition.

Wilfrid Laurier University contributed financial support for the work with an Initiatory Grant and later a Book Preparation Grant.

Throughout the preparation of this edition, I have relied on the knowledge and assistance of librarians and library staff in many institutions, including the Wilfrid Laurier University Library, Dana Porter Library and Doris Lewis Rare Book Room of the University of Waterloo, Robarts Library and Thomas Fisher Rare Book Library of the University of Toronto, the Metropolitan Toronto Reference Library, Bata Library of Trent University, the Library of the Covent Garden Theatre Museum, and the British Library.

Betty Blake and Tim Snider of the New Oxford English Dictionary project at the University of Waterloo generously allowed me to use their computer facilities, and helped me search the *New Oxford English Dictionary* with the software they are developing.

Joanne Buchan and Sandra Wallace, secretaries of the Wilfrid Laurier English Department, gave advice and assistance with many technical questions, as did the staff of Computing Services at Wilfrid Laurier University. The staff of Broadview Press have been unfailingly friendly and helpful. George Kirkpatrick deserves special thanks.

I am especially grateful to the friends and colleagues who helped me immeasurably, in many ways, at different stages of the preparation of the edition, particularly Viviana Comensoli, Veronica Hollinger, Michael Neumann, Manal Stamboulie, Fred Tromly, Eleanor Ty, Lynn Shakinovsky, and Lisa Vargo.

Above all, I thank my husband Martin Ridley Dowding, whose intellectual, editorial and research support has been constant, and greatly appreciated.

Note to the Second Edition

In this edition the bibliography has been updated and a few notes to the "Introduction" have been amended to take into account material published since early 1994. The new material in the Appendices includes two short passages by Behn, early accounts of Behn's life and work by her contemporaries, and an excerpt from *Love in Many Masks*, J.P. Kemble's 1790 adaptation of *The Rover*. I am grateful to Wilfrid Laurier University for its research support.

July, 1997

Introduction

Aphra Behn's Life and Career

Aphra Behn was an extraordinary woman for her time. Her life was not confined by the boundaries normally accepted by seventeenth-century women, whose spheres of influence were the domestic and private. Instead, Behn's was an unusually independent and public life. In her youth she had lived in Surinam, now Dutch Guiana; a few years later she acted as an English agent in the Low Countries during the war between the Dutch and English in the mid-1660s. She is believed to have had a romantic relationship with a lawyer named John Hoyle, an association which has led many critics and biographers to speculate about her sexual life.[1] An outspoken Tory and strong supporter of the monarchy, Behn had some social and professional connections with members of the English court of King Charles II.

Although Behn was not the first woman to publish her writing, she was the first professional woman writer in England. She belonged to the literary and theatrical society of London, where she had a wide acquaintance and was on good terms with professional authors such as John Dryden and Thomas Otway as well as with well-known performers. For nineteen years she made her living as a playwright, translator, poet, and novelist. Her plays were a significant part of the repertory of the Restoration and early eighteenth-century theatre; *The Rover*, her most popular play, was performed in London virtually every year from 1703 to 1750.

Her works remained popular well into the mid eighteenth century, after which her plays, including *The Rover*, virtually disappeared from the stage, partly because their frank analyses of sexual mores were seen as a sign that Behn herself was an indelicate, immoral woman.[2]

Recently there has been a resurgence of interest in Behn's writing, but since the early years of the twentieth century there has been an even greater fascination with her life. Detailed biographical studies have been published by Vita Sackville-West (1928), Walter and Clare Jerrold (1929), George Woodcock (1948), W.J. Cameron (1961), Maureen Duffy (1971), Angeline Goreau (1980), and Sara Heller Mendelson (1987). Behn's life has been treated fictionally in Beth Herst's 1992 play, *A Woman's Comedy*.[3]

Behn's biographers share a common difficulty in their efforts to understand the process by which she became a professional writer. Virtually no documented information about her early life and family circumstances is known to exist. Estimates of her year of birth range from 1640 to as late as 1649. Different late seventeenth-century sources give her birthplace as Canterbury, Sturry, or Wye, all in the county of Kent in southeast England. Her birth name has been given as Johnson or Amis, but searches of baptismal records in Canterbury, Sturry, Wye, and district, where the name Aphra was known in the 1640s, have turned up no entry which unequivocally refers to Behn.[4] When she was earning a living in London's theatrical world her name often appeared in financial and literary documents; nevertheless many elements of Behn's life and career are unknown. Consequently, most studies of Behn's life are characterized by conjecture at many points, a problem which Angeline Goreau acknowledges in the title of her biography, *Reconstructing Aphra: A Social Biography*. Because of the paucity of documents, many commentators are forced to rely on seventeenth-century anecdotes, literary references, and anonymous biographical accounts. To supplement these meager resources, Behn's biographers have used her poetic, dramatic, and fictional works to construct a more detailed, but necessarily speculative, account of her private life. The conflation of Behn's works and life is not a new phenomenon; her love poetry in particular has been read as at least partly autobiographical by many critics since the seventeenth century.[5] I am indebted to Behn's many biographers for the information in the brief account of her life which follows.[6]

The first biographical study of Behn's life is the anonymous "Memoirs of the Life of Mrs. Behn. Written by a Gentlewoman of her Acquaintance." This narrative does not have a great deal of documentary authority, but as the first extant seventeenth-century published account, it has served as the starting point for virtually all subsequent discussions of Behn's personal life. It was published after Behn's death as an introduction to her *Histories and Novels* (London, 1696); a longer version, "The History of the Life and Memoirs of Mrs. Behn" precedes the "Third Edition" of 1698.[7] Although the author of the "Life and Memoirs" signs it "one of the Fair Sex," some critics argue that it might have been written by Charles Gildon, the first editor of Behn's prose works.

According to the memoir, Behn's father, named Johnson, was a gentleman in Canterbury who was appointed Lieutenant General of Surinam by his relative Lord Willoughby. However, the father died on the voyage and, after a short stay, Aphra returned to England, where she married Mr. Behn, a "merchant... of Dutch extraction." A note in the margin of another seventeenth-century document, a manuscript poem by Anne Finch, Duchess of Winchelsea, states that "Mrs. Behn was daughter to a barber, who lived formerly in Wye" (quoted Goreau 9). Another early record, a memoir by Thomas Culpepper, states that Behn was born at Canterbury or Sturry, and that her mother was Culpepper's nurse.[8] However, no uncontroverted documentary evidence has been located regarding Behn's place of birth or family connections.

Another frequently used source for Behn's early life is her prose fiction *Oroonoko* (1688), set in Surinam and narrated in the first person. The female narrator relates that with her mother and brother she accompanies her father to Surinam where he is to be Lieutenant General, but he dies on the voyage. In the colony, she stays in the best house, where she meets a slave whose unsuccessful revolt is the subject of the plot. Since the narrator's account agrees so closely with statements made in the "Memoirs," there has been some debate as to whether *Oroonoko* might have been the source for its details about Behn's Surinam experience.

There is other evidence that Behn actually did spend some time in Surinam (summarized by Goreau 44-45). H.G. Platt demonstrates that many of the narrator's descriptions of the landscape, history, and politics of the colony are accurate. Arguing that *Oroonoko* is partially autobiographical, W.J.

Cameron distinguishes between "the autobiographical comments which are not an integral part of the story of the Negro prince" and those "that are part of the central plot" (Cameron 6) — a fine distinction which he does not discuss in detail. Cameron relies on letters from the colony and other documents to argue that "the external evidence does not destroy the authenticity of Aphra's autobiography, but in fact strengthens it" (13); he dates Behn's arrival in Surinam "towards the end of 1663" and her departure as "before the beginning of March 1663/4" (10). According to Thomas Southerne's "Dedicatory Epistle" to his play *Oroonoko* (1696), adapted from Behn's novel, a friend of hers told Southerne that Behn "always told [Oroonoko's] story more feelingly than she writ it" (Southerne 4). Critical debate continues about how many details of *Oroonoko*, and Behn's other first-person narratives, recount the "real" Behn's life, and how many describe the narrator's character.

Although many biographers state that some time after Behn's departure from Surinam she married Mr. Behn, the "merchant... of Dutch extraction" mentioned in the "Life and Memoirs," no record of this marriage exists; nor does Behn herself mention a marriage or a husband in any known source. Some critics conclude that she may never have married, while others argue that her husband might have died in the plague of 1665.[9] In any case, in 1666 Behn was signing her correspondence "AB" and "A Behn" (Cameron 42,64).

That year, Behn was in Antwerp where she was a spy for the government of Charles II. Her mission was to acquire military and political information from William Scot, who had been in Surinam at the same time as Behn and who was rumored to have been romantically associated with her there.[10] A series of letters between Behn and her contacts at Whitehall — Major Halsall, Thomas Killigrew, and Lord Arlington — evoke a frustrating relationship, in which the correspondents frequently seem to be at cross purposes (many of Behn's later letters include pleas for expense money).[11] Cameron transcribes a letter which includes information about a Dutch plot to sink ships and block the Thames (72-74), but critics disagree on whether the information would have been useful to her contacts at Whitehall at the time she sent it (Cameron 27; Hargreaves "Warning" 203-205). By 1668, Behn was back in London and in debt. Several letters survive in which she asks for money to pay bills incurred in Antwerp. It seems she was committed to debtor's prison (Cameron 33; Goreau 115), but it is not known how long she stayed or on what terms she was released.

Aphra Behn's first play, produced by the Duke's Company at Dorset Garden Theatre in 1670, was *The Forced Marriage*, a theme she would examine in many subsequent works including *The Rover*. What we know of her subsequent career is documented in the records of the production and publication of her numerous plays,[12] fictional prose narratives, translations and poems. In addition, the addresses to readers of her published plays contain some of Behn's public statements about her work and career. Contemporary references to her life and work exist in a number of sources as do some records of her financial transactions. Discussing the latter, Goreau repeatedly notes her generosity to friends even when she herself was in need (see also Mendelson 152).

How Behn became a playwright is unknown. Some commentators suggest that she might have been introduced to the theatre by Thomas Killigrew, who was patentee of one of the two theatres in London at the time as well as one of the officials of King Charles's government with whom Behn corresponded during and after her mission to Antwerp. Whatever help he might have given her, he did not accept her play for production by his own company, the King's Company (she was associated with the Duke's Company). Behn later adapted Killigrew's *Thomaso, or The Wanderer* as a source for *The Rover*. In the "Postscript" to the play, she defends herself from imputed charges of having plagiarized *Thomaso* "which made the booksellers fear some trouble from the proprietor of that admirable play," an indication that she may not have had Killigrew's permission to adapt the play. Behn's defence explicitly challenges her readers to compare her work with *Thomaso*. She writes, "As for the words and characters, I leave the reader to judge and compare 'em with *Thomaso*, to whom I recommend the great entertainment of reading it," a statement which may or may not be sarcastic.

However it was that Behn first became associated with the theatre, she developed into a skilled playwright whose plays were produced frequently during most of her professional career. Her first play, *The Forced Marriage*, was a tragicomedy, but she soon adopted the fashion for comedy, her most successful genre. By the time *The Rover* was first performed and published in 1677, Behn had seen six of her plays produced.[13] Yet *The Rover* first appeared anonymously, with a line in the prologue referring to the author as "he" and "him."

Apparently, Behn did not at first acknowledge the play as her own. There are a number of possible explanations. As a woman playwright, she was an anomalous figure. She wrote her first seven plays (including *The Rover*) without dedications to patrons, an unusually long period for a writer to remain without patronage, and an indication of her status outside "the usual system of contacts and patronage" (Payne 107). At every stage of her career, she was attacked for indelicacy and immorality, both inappropriate for a woman writer.[14] Perhaps the most famous criticism of her is Dryden's. After Behn's death he wrote a letter of advice to Elizabeth Thomas, who had sent him some of her poems:

> you, who write only for your Diversion, may pass your Hours with Pleasure in it, and without Prejudice, always avoiding (as I know you will) the Licenses which Mrs. Behn allowed herself, of writing loosely, and giving, (if I may have leave to say so) some Scandal to the Modesty of her Sex. I confess, I am the last Man who ought, in Justice to arraign her, who have been myself too much a Libertine in most of my poems. (Ward 127)

Although Dryden acknowledges that his approach is similar to Behn's, he criticizes her work as immodest, particularly for a woman writer, and perhaps for a woman reader.

Behn frequently complains that her writing is judged by harsher standards than those applied to men. In the "Prologue" to *The Lucky Chance* (1687) she suggests that women are especially likely to criticize her. She assures women readers that the play has been read by "several Ladys of very great Quality and unquestioned Fame, and received their most favourable Opinion" (Summers 3:187). In "To the Reader" in *Sir Patient Fancy* (1678) she bitterly complains of

> the most unjust and silly aspersion, Woman could invent to cast on Woman; and which only my being a Woman has procured me; *That it was baudy,* the least and most Excusable fault in the Men writers, to whose Plays they all crowd, as if they came to no other end than to hear what they condemn in this: *but from a Woman it was unnaturall.* (Summers 4:7)

Behn also faced charges of plagiarism for using earlier plays as sources for her own, a practice which was widespread in the seventeenth-century theatre. In response to these attacks, Behn frequently points out that her themes and dramatic practices are similar to those of male writers. Perhaps her best-known statement on the topic occurs in the "Preface" to *The Lucky Chance* which tacitly acknowledges that writing is not a feminine activity, but a masculine one:

> All I ask, is the Priviledge [sic] for my Masculine Part the Poet in me... to tread in those successful Paths my Predecessors have so long thriv'd in... If I must not, because of my Sex, have this Freedom, but that you will usurp all to your selves; I lay down my Quill, and you shall hear no more of me... for I am not content to write for a Third day only.[15] I value Fame as much as if I had been born a *Hero*; and if you rob me of that, I can retire from the ungrateful World and scorn its fickle Favours. (Summers 3:187)

In suggesting that writing is the production of "my Masculine Part the Poet," Behn attempts to establish herself as an exception — an extraordinary woman who has within her a "masculine" talent for poetry and heroism, and who asks for the "Priviledge" of exercising those qualities. She offers to stop writing if she "must not, because of my Sex, have this freedom." Yet this relatively submissive statement is qualified by her identification of herself as a "*Hero*" who "can retire" if necessary. The passage shifts from a request for the privilege of expressing her "Masculine Part" to a more confident and assertive description of herself as a "*Hero.*"

Behn's representation of herself as an exception is accurate since, as far as we know, she was the only woman writing professionally at this time.[16] Her public profile as a woman writer had many implications, one of which was her association with other "public women" — especially actresses, with whom she had professional contacts and for whom she wrote dramatic roles. Like women writers, actresses were defining new places for themselves in the public and professional spheres. Behn was thus part of the first generation of English women to participate, as writers and performers, in the representation of women characters in the theatre. Yet at the same time, the places of women as characters and performers were being culturally defined.

During the first part of the seventeenth century, in the public theatre of Shakespeare and other playwrights of the Jacobean and Caroline periods, all women's roles had been played by male performers, usually boys. At court, however, in private performances, women had performed in masques, combinations of music, poetry, dancing and allegorical spectacle. Queen Henrietta Maria, King Charles I's wife, had written and performed in a court masque; Queen Anne, King James's wife, had appeared in non-speaking parts in some of Ben Jonson's masques. However, these exceptional performances by women had been frequently attacked, especially by Puritan commentators (Ferris 65-67). In 1642, after the defeat of royalist forces in the Civil War, Parliament decreed that the theatres in London should close. While some private theatrical and operatic performances were still staged, the flourishing public theatre virtually disappeared until 1660 and the restoration of the monarchy.

In 1660, two theatre companies — the King's and the Duke's — were given charters to perform, and they attempted to recover the repertory and acting traditions which had existed before 1642. At first, women's roles were again played by male actors. But soon after the theatres re-opened, an anonymous woman played Desdemona, becoming the first actress to perform on a public English stage. King Charles II decreed in 1660 that actresses should play women's roles so that plays would be "useful and instructive representations of human life" (quoted Ferris 70), possibly a response to those who claimed that boy actors of women's roles elicited the passions of male spectators. Yet if Restoration actresses were introduced as agents of morality, they were soon blamed for introducing immorality to the theatre. As late as the early twentieth century, theatre historian Allardyce Nicoll expresses the conventional belief that "the male spectators looked upon these actresses as little better than prostitutes" (1:70-71). Certainly many Restoration actresses were the mistresses of courtiers; one of the most famous, Nell Gwyn, had a child by Charles II. But when Nicoll asserts that "the actresses" as a class were responsible for "dragging down the playhouse" (71), his condemnation is overwrought.[17]

Many recent accounts of the Restoration theatre acknowledge the pressures which men in the audience exerted on the actresses, and consider the "immorality" of the theatre as an expression of the cultural context rather than the responsibility of the actresses. Women who became performers in the late seventeenth century were often orphans or alienated from their families. Since women rarely engaged in commerce outside of a family business, almost the only way an unmarried woman could earn a living was as a servant. Acting must have seemed an attractive alternative to service. Once employed, most actresses did not have high salaries, and financial pressures were often acute (Howe 26-29; Langhans, "Actresses" 3-5). The backstage areas of the theatre were public meeting places where men of the court mixed with the performers. Not surprisingly, many actresses, already isolated from traditional family structures in which they were defined as daughters or wives, became involved in sexual relationships with some of these men. Actresses criticized for sexual relations outside marriage were in a problematic position. In public, they did exert some control over their lives and reputations, but the roles they played, which could be limited by typecasting and by stereotypical characterizations, affected their public *personae*. In general, they had relatively little control in sexual relationships with men of high rank.[18]

The seventeenth-century conflation of actress and prostitute further clarifies responses to *The Rover* in particular, to Behn's plays in general, and to her position as a writer. Actresses, like prostitutes, were defined as "public women" and criticized for using their bodies to earn money. Without a clearly defined place in the patriarchal family structure, actresses had to improvise new positions for themselves as public women. Like them, Behn earned her living in the public world, and was exposed to public criticism for behaviour which was acceptable for men. Some critics have suggested that Behn's sympathetic portrayals of prostitutes may indicate that she identifies her position with theirs, particularly in *The Rover*, in which the prostitute Angellica Bianca shares her initials, AB (Diamond 536; Todd *Sign* 1). In the "Postscript" to *The Rover*, a defence against charges that she plagiarized Thomas Killigrew's *Thomaso*, Behn asserts that "the only stolen object is the sign of Angellica," a reference to the three portraits which the courtesan Angellica Bianca hangs in the public square to attract customers in both *Thomaso* and *The Rover*. Elin Diamond suggests that the signs "may... constitute Behn's authorial signature" (536).

But if Behn meant to identify herself with Angellica Bianca, it was a controversial and ambiguous move. Jeslyn Medoff notes that Matthew Prior, who first identified Behn with Angellica Bianca, suggested the writer could "describe the cunning of a Jilting Whore" from experience (quoted Medoff 34). Robert Gould addressed a satire to Behn which concluded, "For Punk and Poetess agree so Pat,/You cannot be This and not be That" (quoted Diamond 520). These hostile seventeenth-century identifications of Behn with her prostitute character obviously have different aims than do more sympathetic recent discussions. Catherine Gallagher argues that Behn consciously "introduced to the world of English letters the professional woman writer as a newfangled whore" (66) in order to explore the simultaneous liberty and confinement the stage offered women. But the suggestion that the woman writer and the prostitute occupy similar cultural positions is not explicit in all of Behn's work. Indeed, the many prefaces in which she criticizes the double standards applied to her as a woman writer suggest that rather than wishing to be identified with her prostitute characters, Behn was eager to be judged by the same standards as male writers.

Ironically, there were already conventions in place which required women in the theatre to mask as men. The introduction of actresses to the English stage eliminated the practice of boys playing women's roles,[19] but the fascination with crossdressing was so deeply ingrained in pre-Restoration theatrical practice, that it resurfaced in what is known as the "breeches part." This is an adaptation of the female-page plot device found in many Elizabethan and Jacobean plays in which a woman character, played by a boy actor, is disguised as a boy. In many of the Restoration comedies which include the motif of the "breeches part", there is little plot motivation for the disguise, and minimal self-consciousness or reflection on the part of the character who disguises.

Behn frequently employs the convention; in *The Rover*, for example, Hellena appears in boy's clothes. Frances M. Kavenik suggests that Behn employed "breeches parts" in her plays to show that "women could share the libertine philosophy with men and experience its liberating effects, in much the same way as she was able to compete on relatively equal terms with the best male playwrights of her time" (190-91). Kavenik's optimistic assessment of Behn's ability to be accepted as a typical playwright is not shared by commentators who see the crossdressed female figure's relation to masculine and feminine as problematic. Crossdressing implies the transgression of boundaries which are traditionally regarded as fixed; Behn's plea for acceptance of "my masculine part, the Poet" demonstrates her awareness of the difficulty of acceptance. Jessica Munns suggests that as a writer Behn "double-dresses, and insists that her audience/readers accept her female gender and her right to a freedom of expression and range of topics hitherto limited to male literary production" ("Double Right" 195). The critical debate over the implications of Behn's anomalous place as a woman playwright frequently returns to the similarities of actress, prostitute, and writer as public women, and to the ways in which Behn's situation can be illuminated by comparison with the public women for whom and about whom she wrote.

Behn's last years, in which she produced many of her fictional prose narratives, were marked by illness and poverty, but also by tremendous productivity. The cause of her death is not known. She is buried in the cloister of Westminster Abbey under a plain black stone which inscribes her date of death as April 16, 1689, and commemorates her with the lines:

> Here lies a proof that wit can never be
> Defence enough against mortality.

Sources of *The Rover*

Like many other Restoration dramatists who relied on the body of plays written before 1642 for plot ideas and character types that could be adapted for contemporary audiences,[20] Behn was often inspired by earlier plays. Since she was writing for a specific and well-defined courtly audience, it is not surprising that her plays conformed to fashions in contemporary drama. But while the dramatic genres Behn employed were familiar,[21] she presented conventional dramatic situations from unusual perspectives.

The Rover falls into the general category of Restoration comedy, which relies on sexual innuendo, intrigue, and wit. More specifically, the play has been categorized as one of the last "sex comedies" popular in the 1670s (Scouten and Hume 56). These comedies often focus on the rake, or libertine, who criticizes marriage as an institution which controls sexuality and pleasure in the interest of property. But *The Rover* has links with a number of other genres and styles. It employs many of the conventions of Spanish comedy, which is characterized by complicated plots full of intrigue and disguise in which an imprisoned girl wins the right to choose her lover or husband (Burns 15). In addition, *The Rover* draws on early seventeenth-century comic genres. As we shall see, Behn adapts a model from Shakespeare's *As You Like It* to structure the relationships between women in the high and low plots. In the "Postscript" to *The Rover*, Behn acknowledges a debt to

Richard Brome's comic play *The Novella* (1632). But the most important source for *The Rover* is Thomas Killigrew's *Thomaso, or The Wanderer*, published in 1663 and probably written in the mid-1650s. Many of the episodes in *The Rover* are adaptations of scenes from Killigrew's play, which is in turn indebted to earlier texts, including Thomas Middleton's citizen comedy *Blurt Master Constable* (1601), Ben Jonson's *Volpone* (1607) and others.[22] *Thomaso* is a long, episodic prose drama which Killigrew seems to have planned to produce, but for which no records of performance exist. The hero of *Thomaso*, like its author, is a royalist supporter of the future Charles II who was exiled to Europe during the interregnum, the period when England was ruled by Parliament under Oliver Cromwell. Behn takes so many ideas for plot, setting, and action from *Thomaso*, that she feels obliged to defend herself against charges that the play "was *Thomaso* altered... That I have stolen some hints from it, may be a proof that I valued it more than to pretend to alter it" ("Postscript" to *The Rover*).

Behn's response here is ingenuous, for a great deal of the situation and plot material in *The Rover* is derived from *Thomaso*. However, she adds dramatic form to Killigrew's rambling and often unfocussed ten-act play, which Alfred Harbage has called "about the least stageworthy of Killigrew's productions" (102). In contrast, Behn's five-act play shows sophisticated dramatic structure and stagecraft. She certainly took more from *Thomaso* than her "Postscript" acknowledges. Yet *The Rover* also displays some of Behn's characteristic preoccupations, in particular the perspectives of women characters on love and marriage. In Killigrew's play, a romantic heroine named Serulina evades a repressive brother and several would-be rapists before she is married to the man of her choice, Thomaso the Wanderer. But the romantic heroine is not central to the play, for much of the action focusses on the sexual adventures of a group of exiled English cavaliers, including Thomaso, with women who include the prostitutes Angellica Bianca, a courtesan willing to experiment with a free love relationship with Thomaso, and Lucetta. Later, Thomaso rejects the female libertine's way of life to marry the virginal Serulina.[23]

In *The Rover* Behn shifts the focus from male to female characters. She develops the character of Angellica Bianca to illustrate the problematic position of a prostitute who has a place in society as long as she treats herself as a commodity but who is marginalized if she succumbs to romantic love. In the interplay between high and low plots, the play illustrates the similarities in the positions of prostitutes and marriageable young women. Behn splits Killigrew's romantic heroine Serulina into two sisters — Florinda, who resembles Serulina, and Hellena, a witty heroine who pursues the man of her choice and wins him as a husband. Behn also adds a cousin, Valeria, who becomes active in the plot late in the play. By doubling the lovers in the high plot, Behn contrasts the romantic and relatively passive "serious" lovers with the playful and witty lovers Hellena and Willmore. Thomaso, a complicated character who is alternately romantic and rakish, is split into two psychologically simpler characters: Belvile, and Willmore the Rover, who is less introspective than is Killigrew's Wanderer.

While *Thomaso* criticizes, from the perspective of the male characters, the economic structures which regulate sexuality, Behn is concerned with many of the same issues from the point of view of women characters.[24] In adapting Killigrew's plot in a way which clarifies the sexual double standards with which women struggle, she draws on the structural and thematic patterns of Shakespeare's *As You Like It*. In each play a pair of women characters who are confidantes and companions resist the power of male family members over them. The more independent woman character disguises herself as a boy, and in disguise develops a witty relationship with the man she loves. The quieter woman character has a more conventional, romantic relationship. Yet while she relies on characters and situations developed by Shakespeare, Behn makes a number of modifications. In *As You Like It* there is an accepted and unexamined class distinction between the women characters of the high and low plots. In *The Rover* Behn stresses the class distinctions between virgins and prostitutes, and many of the women characters discuss the paradoxes and double binds of gender and economic relations. The divisions between virgins and prostitutes have great social force. Angellica, the prostitute who tries to revise her place in the class/gender structure, is excluded by all characters from the marriages at the end of the play. By insisting on marriage, the virginal Hellena returns to the traditional institutions she criticized at the beginning. In *The Rover* the ideologies surrounding class and gender, and the conventions of the comic genre, require virgins and wives to remain in separate worlds from prostitutes.

The Rover: Critical Issues

The Rover, Behn's most successful play, skilfully incorporates intrigue, disguise and slapstick into a complicated plot which ends in marriage. The central male character Willmore, the Rover, is a rake or libertine, a familiar dramatic type.[25] The rake, who exists outside the structures and mores of organized society, seeks liberty and pleasure; he often makes explicit criticisms of the institution of marriage because it suppresses sexual desire by incorporating it into the economic system. The heroine and rake are attracted to each other's love of pleasure and wit. In the fifth-act conversion typical of the genre, she persuades him to marry her in spite of his former critique of marriage as an institution.

One of the unusual elements of *The Rover* is that it presents issues usually introduced by the rake from the perspective of women characters. *The Rover* opens with a discussion by virginal women of their positions in the marriage economy. (The scene includes Hellena's vivid speech describing the disgust of a young woman at the thought of consummating a forced marriage to an older man.) Later Angellica Bianca argues that wives and prostitutes have much in common, in that they are treated as commodities in a system in which women are objects of economic exchange. In plot, structure, and characterization, the early parts of the play expose the sexual double standards by which women are judged, but these inherent contradictions in sexual and economic relations are blunted by setting and plot development.

Setting the play in Naples in the 1650s, Behn evokes a non-specific "exotic" foreign setting and places the events in a misty past. By 1677, the royalist cavaliers who had been in exile twenty years earlier were established as Tories in England; in retrospect, the instability and poverty of the interregnum is transformed into cheerful bohemianism. Willmore, the Rover, is a romanticized and comic figure of the libertine cavalier, seen from a nostalgic distance. (The character was so popular with contemporary audiences that Behn wrote a sequel in 1681, *The Second Part of The Rover*.)

As the early scenes make clear, there are three options for women in the society represented in *The Rover* — marriage, the convent, or prostitution. Marriages are arranged by fathers or brothers for their own political or financial benefit — in *The Rover* Florinda's brother Pedro tries marry Florinda to his own friend rather than to their father's candidate for her husband. After marriage, the wife moves from being controlled by the men of her family to being controlled by her husband. Hellena's description of Florinda's future role as a wife dwells on her confinement in the country and in the bedroom. Hellena's own fate is to become a nun. The nun's position, like the wife's, is arranged by her family, and has some elements in common with marriage — she is given a dowry to take to the convent, where she is called a bride of Christ. In the play, Hellena characterizes the nun's life by images of confinement such as the grate and the cell.

The young women conclude their discussions of their oppressed and confined situations in an act of resistance — they go out in disguise to join the carnival celebrations which are in progress.[26] Since everyone wears costumes and masks at carnival, Florinda disguises herself in a generic carnival habit, while Hellena becomes a gypsy. The anonymity made possible by carnival disguise functions, temporarily, to free the young women from the family. Disguise drives the plot in many ways, and gives the characters opportunities to meet the men they will marry at the end of the play. After first appearing as a gypsy, Hellena adopts the conventional "breeches part" when she appears as a boy, a disguise which is not anticipated in previous discussions. Hellena's ease with male disguise follows the Restoration theatrical convention of the "breeches part," which the heroine uses not as a way to examine gender roles but as a means to an end. Hellena does not mention any strategies needed to play a male convincingly, but exploits the possibilities of the disguise without drawing attention to it. As a boy, she brings messages to Willmore from his beloved (herself); her observations of Willmore's actions function to give her insight into his character, though she makes no explicit acknowledgment that she has learned anything else as a result of her crossgender roleplay. But in dressing as a boy, Hellena avoids some of the problems encountered by masked women, for she is not, as they are, constantly approached for sex.

The mask is a powerful image in Restoration drama.[27] In the 1660s, some women began to wear masks when they attended the theatre. But when prostitutes also began to wear masks, the distinctions between prostitutes and "respectable women" became blurred. The mask became a sign of the prostitute, but a sign which, with its offer of anonymity, could offer some freedom from conventional roles for any woman who wore it; Lesley Ferris suggests that the experience of wearing masks might have been not only "liberating" but also "subversive" (74).

In *The Rover* masks are often both subversive and liberating for the women characters; on the other hand, they also place some of the women in dangerous situations because of the association of the mask with the prostitute. The difficulty of distinguishing between "respectable women" and prostitutes is a recurrent theme in the play, and is made explicit in the first carnival scene, which opens with a group of exiled English royalists meeting in the streets of Naples. The English cavaliers watch in amusement as masked women pass by wearing, pinned to their clothing, papers which say, "Roses for every month." Belvile glosses the signs to mean, "They are, or would have you think, they're courtesans, who here in Naples are to be hired for the month." Belvile's awareness that the women may be courtesans, or may merely be masquerading as courtesans, prepares for a number of discussions and situations in which the parallels between "respectable women" and prostitutes as commodities are represented. So frequently is this subject articulated that Elin Diamond has suggested that Behn's theme in *The Rover* is "the commodification of women in the marriage market" (524).[28] The play stresses the ways in which the prostitute's economic position parallels that of the wife's in the patriarchal family. A prostitute who has a protector or a pimp is enclosed in a structure in which her place as commodity is stable and recognizable. At the beginning of the play Angellica Bianca is alone, her previous protector having died. She is actively looking for a replacement, rich enough to pay her a thousand crowns a month. The economic relationship between courtesan and protector parallels that between husband and wife, yet its temporary aspect gives Angellica more control than a wife. Angellica is able to choose her purchaser — something that women who are destined to be wives do not always have the power to do. And it is Angellica who makes explicit the similarities between the situations of wife and prostitute in the long scene in which she and Willmore debate the relationships between love and money. Angellica eloquently deplores the double standards employed by men, but she is affected by Willmore's critique of her as a mercenary; her attraction to him induces her to agree to bypass the usual exchange of money for sex in the interests of an ideal of free love.

Angellica, like the virgins of the play, is subject to what her servant and advisor Moretta calls the "disease of our sex," romantic love. Love, like a disease, weakens Angellica. When she succumbs to Willmore's argument that love ought to be given rather than sold, she gives up her independence and becomes vulnerable both emotionally and economically. She not only gives herself to Willmore, but she gives him money also. Having gained this prize, Willmore immediately shifts his attention to the pursuit of Hellena, whom he has previously met in her gypsy disguise.

While it is against Willmore's principles of free love to marry, at the end of the play he abrogates these principles in order to marry the witty virgin Hellena, something he would not do for the prostitute Angellica. Driven by jealousy and unrequited love, Angellica threatens Willmore with a pistol, but she is easily disarmed by Antonio, Willmore's rival for possession of her. As a result of her vulnerability to romantic love, Angellica Bianca moves from a position of strength in an economic system which recognizes her value as a commodity to a position of dependence in an economy of emotion. After she falls in love, she changes from an articulate and intelligent character, aware of the ways in which economic and sexual systems interact to control women, to a stereotype of the jealous and emotional woman. Ultimately, she is a melodramatic figure who is written out of the play and hustled offstage before the questions she has raised can be fully resolved.

If Angellica is the clichéd whore with a heart (though not of gold), the other prostitute, Lucetta, is a mercenary "jilting wench." When she robs and humiliates Blunt, who has believed her to be attracted to him, his anger unleashes his hatred of all women. Prostitutes who are mercenary, like Lucetta, may gain money and keep control, but they bring the rage of their victims on other women. At several points the plot shows men's resentment against prostitutes, and when the boundaries between prostitutes and "respectable" women are blurred, all women become potential targets of rage.

The vulnerability of women who are not under the protection of men is represented at numerous points in *The Rover* by attempted rapes.[29] Florinda, the prototypical romantic heroine, is especially targeted. Before the play begins she is rescued by Belvile from soldiers invading Pamplona. During the play she is twice threatened with rape. When she is waiting for Belvile in the garden at night, the drunken Willmore stumbles into her and argues that since her garden gate was open, she must have meant to entice him. She is rescued by Belvile and Frederick, who condemn Willmore for drunkenness and bungling but not for his violent struggle with Florinda. Later, when Florinda is escaping her brother she runs into Belvile's house wearing carnival disguise and mask. The only person present is Blunt, bitterly angry at his betrayal by Lucetta, and determined to beat and to rape the next woman he sees. While Blunt is threatening Florinda, Frederick returns and amusedly decides to join Blunt. Florinda persuades the men to delay their proposed rape by giving them a diamond and promising to prove her identity as a respectable woman. The jewel makes Frederick pause, since he does not want "to be taken for raping a maid of quality when we only mean to ruffle a harlot." Later, virtually all the male characters, including Florinda's brother, draw swords for the first chance at her. Although Belvile arrives, he cannot think of a way to stop the men from chasing her around the room without revealing her identity to her brother. Florinda is saved not by her fiancé, but by the wit of her cousin Valeria. When her identity as a respectable woman betrothed to Belvile is revealed, her future husband's friends make only perfunctory apologies, and Florinda does not seem to expect more.

The difficulty Blunt and Frederick have in telling a "maid of quality" from a "harlot" is shared by all the men in the play. Blunt mistakes the prostitute Lucetta for a rich wife who loves him; Willmore mistakes Florinda for a prostitute; the masquerading women wear papers on their clothing "as if whores." The boundaries separating "woman of quality" and "whore" have been destabilized. Yet the implications of this instability are not developed. Angellica Bianca is emotionally weakened when she stops selling herself and gives herself for love, but the sympathy which the character begins to evoke is undercut when she becomes jealous and threatens violence. In the end, all the problems previously raised by Angellica are erased, since her challenge to Willmore is not resolved.

In this comedy, which, conventionally, ends in marriage, the figure of the prostitute cannot be integrated. Marriage is seen as a problem by the women of quality at the beginning of the play; by the end, marriage is a solution to a problem, though not an ideal one. Hellena pragmatically chooses marriage over Willmore's offer of free love because she recognizes that no matter how bad marriage might be, the hazard of being unmarried is greater. Sleeping with Willmore outside of marriage will lead, she argues, to "a pack of troubles and a cradle full of repentance"; to avoid it, she calls for "old gaffer Hymen" to regularize the union. Hellena's disguise has given her insight into Willmore's inconstancy, but her insistence on marriage seems less a strategy to control him than a way to protect herself from the consequences of being defined as a "whore."

Hellena's utilitarian attitude to marriage can be contrasted to that of Belvile and Florinda, who adhere to a romanticized view of woman as a prize to be won by a man's prowess. They first fall in love after Belvile saves her at the siege of Pamplona; later Belvile fights a duel in disguise and wins Florinda again. When he asserts, "She's mine by conquest, sir, I won her by the sword" he speaks not to her but to her brother; the focus is not on his love for her or her choice of him, but on his skill at winning a wife. The early parts of the play define him as a protector of his beloved, yet no character comments on Belvile's ineffectual presence when Florinda is being chased by his friends. The third marriage, that of Valeria and Frederick, is a conventional dramatic one, the result of an immediate attraction which has not been analyzed or tested. No explicit attention is drawn to the problematic nature of any of these marriages, except perhaps in the final couplet, which refers to "the storms o' the marriage bed."

Critical appraisals of *The Rover*, like other developments in Behn criticism, have until recently focussed on her life. Frederick Link's survey of Behn's body of work (1968) concisely categorizes and summarizes her many literary productions. Since the early 1980s there has been a noticeable increase in critical discussions, though many of these studies still have a primary interest in Behn's professional and sexual life. Most of the criticism is devoted to her fiction, with a decided focus on *Oroonoko*. A rapidly growing critical debate on her poetry has been encouraged by the publication of Germaine Greer's edition of *The Uncollected Verse of Aphra Behn* (1989) and Janet Todd's edition of Behn's *Poetry* (1992). Behn's plays are often considered briefly in general discussions of women writers or Restoration drama. A relatively small but rapidly growing body of criticism analyzes individual plays, especially *The Lucky Chance*, *The Widow Ranter*, and *The Rover*. Some insightful discussions of *The Rover* are included in two recent anthologies, *Curtain Calls: British and American Women and the Theatre, 1660-1820*, edited by Mary Ann Schofield and Cecilia Macheski (1991) and *Rereading Aphra Behn: History, Theatre and Criticism*, edited by Heidi Hutner (1993).

Critical responses to *The Rover* generally acknowledge that there are a number of tensions and contradictions inherent in the play. In their discussions of the extent to which the play criticizes its society, critics give different emphasis to the beginning of the play and its conclusion, to the explicit and the implicit, and to conventional and unconventional elements. The plot includes duels, robberies, and attempted rapes; characters make casual antisemitic slurs; anticatholic comments acknowledge the inquisition in the background. Laura Brown argues that "the form implies a condemnation of that very society whose standards constitute the terms of its action" (61), while Jessica Munns suggests that the content, not the form, is the source of social criticism, when she mentions "uncomfortable moments that throw off-balance the move to a happy ending" ("Double Right" 201.) The "uncomfortable moment" most often discussed is Angellica's final scene in which she threatens Willmore with a pistol, a scene which Link suggests does "not quite fit the comic world of the play" (*Rover* Introduction xvi). Other "uncomfortable moments" include antisemitic slurs used in conversation[30] as well as the proposed rapes of Florinda, but these problems are rarely explored in criticism of the play.

Another concern is how to define and understand Behn's unusual portrayal of male and female characters. Some critics prefer to define her as a proto-femininist or feminist writer (Langdell 110). However, this perspective is qualified by arguments such as Nancy Cotton's that she represents male libertine characters much less critically than do Etherege and Wycherly ("Pattern Hero" 215-218). While Cotton suggests that Behn's interest in writing "from her own gender perspective" ("Pattern Hero" 217) might account for these relatively uncritical male representations, their characterizations put into question the seriousness with which we are to interpret the women characters' criticisms of marriage. The women's complaints about marriage focus on their own places in the social structure; male control of the institution is not emphasized so much as the position of women as pawns within it. The play opens with a sympathetic portrayal of women subject to male control, but there is throughout an indulgent tolerance of individual male characters. Although all of the men except Belvile propose rape, not even the women criticize the practice. Blunt's angry and explicit statements of his desire to beat and to rape women in revenge for his treatment by Lucetta are incongruous elements in a character who is introduced as a dim-witted comic butt. And Willmore's drunkenness and pursuit of all women are represented as endearing foibles. (Belvile does criticize Willmore, primarily for his tendency to interfere drunkenly with Belvile's secret meetings with Florinda.) While Willmore makes many speeches attacking mercenary relationships, his practice is not as honourable as his arguments would suggest. He may not be explicitly seeking a rich woman, but when he finds one he does not hesitate to exploit her financial resources.[31]

Cotton's argument that Behn "seems unconcerned about these masculine doubts" ("Pattern Hero" 217) implies that Behn is more interested in the women than the men. Alternately, the relatively unproblematic portrayal of Willmore and the other male characters might be interpreted as part of a realistic or unsentimental representation of a culture characterized by violence and discrimination. The violent setting can also be seen as exotic local colour introduced by a playwright who knows what her audience wants.[32] Whether or not *The Rover* is most striking for its protofeminist perspective on women characters in which, as Jaqueline Pearson argues, "images of female power are...most emphatic" (154) or is characterized by "a restoration of patriarchal authority" (Hutner 103),[33] its many tensions and contradictions make it a fascinating play.

Stage History

The first recorded production of *The Rover* was at the Dorset Garden Theatre on 24 March 1677, though it is not known if this was the première of the play (*London Stage* 1:256). The play was very popular in the London theatre for almost eighty years. It was presented at court in 1680, 1685, 1687, and 1690, was performed in London theatres virtually every year until 1750, and remained in the repertoire until 1757.

The first edition of the play, published in 1677, includes a cast list which names a number of popular actors. The two co-managers of the theatre, Thomas Betterton (1635-1710) and William Smith (died 1695), had key roles. Betterton, who played the romantic Belvile, was famous as an actor and manager. Mary Betterton, née Saunderson (c. 1637-1712) performed Florinda, Belvile's beloved.

William Smith took the role of Willmore, the Rover. Though Smith's name is not now as famous as Betterton's, he was a respected actor whose first documented appearance on the London stage was as Antonio in *The Duchess of Malfi* in 1662. Hellena was one of Elizabeth Barry's (c. 1658-1713) early roles — she later became famous, particularly for creating leading roles in the tragedies of Thomas Otway. Blunt was performed by the comedian Cave Underhill (c. 1634-c.1710). This was a popular role for Underhill; he performed some of Blunt's scenes in a booth at Greenwich as late as 1710 (*Dictionary of National Biography*).

The key part of Angellica Bianca was played by Mrs. Anne Quin (fl. 1660-1683), who had earlier appeared as Mrs. Anne Marshall. The first cast list, which was reproduced in many later editions, including the 1915 Montague Summers' edition, assigns the part of Angellica Bianca to "Mrs. Gwin," and many records indicate that Nell Gwyn herself played the role.[34] But since Anne Quin is variously identified in contemporary records and cast lists as Mrs Quin, Quinn, Quyn, Guin, Gwin and Wyn, not surprisingly there has been some confusion of the two actresses. Although Nell Gwyn had performed in some of Behn's early plays, and Behn had dedicated *The Feigned Courtesans* to her in 1679, Gwyn left the stage after 1671, six years before *The Rover* was produced.

The choice of Anne Quin for Angellica Bianca is interesting, since it seems that she had also been Killigrew's choice for the role in a planned production of Behn's source for *The Rover, Thomaso, or The Wanderer. Thomaso* was published in 1663, after Killigrew acquired the patent for the Bridges Street Theatre, but without prologue, epilogue, or actors' names in the list of *dramatis personae*, suggesting that it had not been acted before publication. *The London Stage* suggests that when Killigrew was manager of the King's Company he "prepared *Thomaso* for production in the autumn of 1664," with an intended cast that included Mrs. Anne Marshall (later Quin) as Angellica Bianca and Nell Gwyn as Paulina, but that "no notice of production exists" (1:84). *A Biographical Dictionary of London Actors* suggests that Quin "probably" acted the role in *Thomaso* (12:243). When Behn wrote *The Second Part of the Rover* in 1681, apparently by popular demand, several of the original cast reprised their roles as Anne Quin may have done between *Thomaso* and *The Rover*. It was common practice for performers in sequels to play the same characters they had created (Holland 67). Cave Underhill again played Blunt, and Smith played the romantic cavalier Willmore for the second time. Years later Willmore was his first role after returning from service in an army that supported James II until his abdication in 1688. In supporting an exiled Stuart king, Smith's life seems to have imitated his character's.

Elizabeth Barry could not reprise the important role of Hellena in *The Second Part of The Rover*, since that character has died; early in Act 1 of *Rover 2*, Willmore briefly mentions his wife's death at sea. Willmore, however, is not changed by marriage or by Hellena's death, for he is soon pursuing a courtesan named La Nuche, played by Barry. In *Rover 2* the love affair between Willmore and the courtesan is more "successful" for Willmore since his arguments in favour of free love, made to Angellica Bianca and then to Hellena in *The Rover*, are accepted by La Nuche, who at the end of the play pledges herself to live with him in spite of poverty and risk. There is no character analogous to Hellena, who points out in *The Rover* the extent to which an ideal of free love carries many possible costs for women which are not borne by men.[35] While many Restoration playwrights had close connections with the companies for which they wrote their plays and knew the actors with whom the play would be cast, it is difficult to be sure what control Behn might have had over the casting of Barry as La Nuche. Assuming that she "took care over the repeated casting," Peter Holland argues that the audience's

> perception of underlying structure, the inevitability of a match between Smith and Mrs. Barry, is allowed to carry over between the parts. Mrs. Behn can profit from this to underline the alternatives: Willmore is forced to marry Hellena but his bargain with La Nuche is achieved without marriage — a reflection of the degradation of the heroine into a prostitute. . .

and of the increasingly extra-social position of the rake in the comedies of the 1680s. (67-68)

Like many sequels, *The Second Part of the Rover* was not as successful as the original had been, nor does it seem to have been performed after its first production in 1681.

There are indications that some of the situations in *The Rover* were increasingly seen as risqué, particularly after Jeremy Collier's *Short View of the Immorality and Profaneness of the English Stage* in 1698 helped to define, as well as to encourage, changing standards in language and situations considered appropriate for theatrical representation. A promptbook of the first edition of *The Rover*, which Edward A. Langhans believes dates from the 1720s, indicates a number of cuts of sexually explicit lines and episodes (144-148). Scouten and Hume note that in the 1750s and 1760s there were many hostile attacks on what they call "the older comedies" by "*writers who attended the theatre and supported the drama*" (79; their emphasis), and that in the 1760s and 1770s many of these plays were performed only in altered versions (80).

A report in *The London Chronicle* (22-24 February, 1757) of a production of *The Rover* at Covent Garden illustrates the shift in audience response. The ladies in the theatre "are first alarmed; then the Men stare: The Women put up their Fans" when "One of the Personages of the Drama takes off his Breeches in the Sight of the Audience," a reference to the scene in which Blunt undresses in Lucetta's chamber. The account goes on to note that the play was written "in the dissolute Days of Charles the Second; and that Decency at least is, or ought to be, demanded at present" (quoted Agate 21). Montague Summers' account of the same production, which he dates as 19 February 1757, stresses that Mr. Shuter, the actor playing Blunt, did not improvise new and more shocking business here, but "exactly followed the old realistic traditions and in Act III as the business requires he undressed to his very shirt and drawers" (190). Summers adds that in the scene in which Blunt climbs from the sewer the actor "resorted to the original methods and covered himself with chawed gingerbread" (191). Perhaps it was the faithfulness of this production to stage tradition, and its distance from the increasingly popular sentimental drama, which made it seem inappropriate in 1757. This is the last recorded performance of *The Rover* in London until 1790, when John Philip Kemble presented a revision of the play called *Love in Many Masks* (see Appendix C).

Kemble's alterations of *The Rover* indicate that the play was increasingly seen as morally suspect. Kemble shortened the five acts to three, and in the process cut out much of the dialogue and action pertaining to sex. Hellena's speech about the horror of forced marrage is removed, and the rape plot against Florinda is merely implied. Hellena makes some very highminded speeches about honour ("My birth, my breeding and pride raise me far above the coarse interchange of mere convenient pleasures — I offer my heart for yours" [*Love in Many Masks* 23]). Like Hellena, Willmore is more refined and calm than he is in *The Rover*; in particular, he is less often drunk and chasing women, hence more worthy of a woman like Hellena. The Blunt episodes are also softened; Lucetta's trap door drops him into another street, rather than into the sewer, and she tells her colleagues that she is trying to teach him a lesson about vanity, an ostensibly moral purpose absent from Behn's play. The final lines of Kemble's version substitute optimism about marriage and honour for Willmore's cynicism about "the storms o' th' marriage bed."

Love in Many Masks is a much simpler and politer play than *The Rover*. Although the production, and some individual performances, were praised for their humour, a newspaper review published 9 March 1790 nevertheless complains that "the ideas are constantly indelicate, and the language frequently gross". The reviewer especially objects to a play with a courtesan as a central character, and suggests that the adapter ought to have eliminated Angellica Bianca entirely.[36] *Love in Many Masks* was performed only a few times; it had eight performances in March 1790 and one in October of that year. After Kemble's failed attempt to present the play in a relatively sanitized version, *The Rover* virtually disappeared from the stage until the late 1970s.

Most of the few recent productions of *The Rover* have been by university or small alternative theatre groups; the exception is the Royal Shakespeare Company's revival in 1986 of an adapted version. A review of a production at the University of Illinois at Chicago Circle in 1979 praises the company for stressing physicality over a conventional comedy of manners style (Hume 412-13); the Folger Theatre Group's production in Washington in 1982 was deemed "surprisingly sophisticated" (Gusso, *NYT* Jan 14, 1982:C17). The play was also performed by the Upstream Theatre in London in July 1984 (Carlson 152-154).

For its production at the Swan Theatre in 1986 and then at the Mermaid Theatre in London in 1987, the RSC director and adaptor John Barton incorporated some passages from Killigrew's *Thomaso*. Barton changed the setting of the play to the West Indies, making an explicit link between sexual double standards and slavery not found in the Behn text. He also added numerous lines in which women characters explicitly express sexual desire. While the production received generally favourable reviews, some academic commentators have been less approving of Barton's interpolations from Killigrew and his other alterations of Behn's text. Nancy Copeland argues that the passages from Killigrew function to represent relationships between men and women "more crudely than in Behn's play" ("Reproducing *The Rover*" 51), in particular by making Angellica Bianca "a conventional, and therefore easily recognizable, prostitute figure" ("Reproducing *The Rover*" 52). Jessica Munns suggests that "in seeking recognition of Behn's relevance for today, Barton obscures the points at which we can find genuine parallels between Behn's texts and our social contexts... [and] obscures the points at which Behn's values and moral patterns are not our own" ("Barton" 19; see also Carlson 155-56). An American production of *The Rover* at the Williamstown Theatre Festival followed the RSC innovation of setting the play in the West Indies and altering the text; the reviewer found the second half "tedious" (Rev. Frank Rich *NYT* July 27, 1987:C18).[37]

While *The Rover* may be returning to the theatrical repertoire, the Royal Shakespeare Company's decision not to perform it without interpolation and revision suggests that the play continues to have the power to challenge conventional expectations. The successful revivals of Behn's text, however,

indicate that *The Rover* still has the potential to reward production.

Notes

1. Many discussions of Behn's sexuality and relationship with
Hoyle use her novels and poetry as evidence of her inner life,
but do not problematize the relationship between art and life.
Hoyle was involved in several duels, was charged and acquitted
of sodomy, and ultimately killed in a knife fight. Most of
Behn's biographers, including Sackville-West, Woodcock,
Duffy, Goreau and Mendelson read Behn's *Love-Letters to a
Gentleman* (1684) as autobiographical records of her
relationship with Hoyle, and must therefore speculate whether
he was homosexual or bisexual. See also Salvaggio's suggestion
that Behn's heterosexual desire "is undermined by the
homosexual and/or homosocial" (257).

2. For a discussion of Behn's literary reputation in the
seventeenth and eighteenth centuries, see Medoff (33-35).

3. Herst's play was produced at Tarragon Theatre, Toronto, in
April 1992 and at the University of Guelph, Ontario, 29
November to 4 December 1993.

4. Most biographies give a probable birthdate of 1640, partly
because a now discredited baptismal reference to an Aphra
Amis born in that year was once thought to be Behn's.
However, Duffy strongly argues for 1640 (Duffy 16-23) while
Mendelson believes that references to Behn's youth at the time
of the voyage to Surinam mean that she cannot have been
born before the late 1640s (116). In a recent article, Jane Jones
agrees with Duffy that Behn was "likely" born to Bartholomew
Johnson and Elizabeth Denham in 1640 in Harbledown, near
Canterbury (290). In her 1996 biography, *The Secret Life of
Aphra Behn*, Janet Todd accepts Jones's argument.

5. Behn's poems are often read singly and autobiographically.
For example, many critics read "The Disappointment" as a
poem about Behn's dismay at a male lover's impotence, while

Arlene Stiebel interprets Behn's "To the Fair Clarinda, who made Love to me, Imagin'd More than Woman" as evidence that Behn is a "lesbian author" (161-163).

6.   The biographies disagree greatly on the significance of many fragments of information, but I do not analyze these disputes in detail, since my focus is on the parts of Behn's life and dramatic career which are documented, especially those which are relevant to a reading of *The Rover*.

7.   Because no second edition is extant, some bibliographers cast doubt on its designation. (See excerpts from the "Life and Memoirs" in Appendix B.) W.J. Cameron discusses the "Memoir" in *New Light on Aphra Behn* (14-17; 87-100). For a detailed discussion of the differences between subsequent versions of the early biographical accounts of Behn see Robert Adams Day, "Aphra Behn's First Biography."

8.   The relevant part of Culpepper's memoir is reproduced by Mendelson (116). Duffy relies on this document in her discussion of Behn's birth (19), as does Jones, while Mendelson argues that it is inaccurate (116). See also Goreau's discussion (11-13).

9.   Hargreaves' "A Case for Mr. Behn" is the most specific defence of the existence of a husband. See also James Fitzmaurice's "Aphra Behn and the *Abraham's Sacrifice* case." Goreau argues that since there are no records attacking Behn's right to call herself Mrs. Behn, she was probably known by her contemporaries to have been married (85). No documentary evidence is known which would support the theory that "Mr. Behn" died in the plague.

10.   Scot, a political exile, had military associations with the Dutch army. All of Behn's recent biographers discuss Behn's rumoured relationship with Scot in Surinam and her dealings with him in Antwerp. Todd and McKee draw on unpublished letters of Thomas Corney, another English agent, to outline some of the intrigue and double dealing in which Behn was involved. They conclude that Behn's mission was less

important — and less secret — than she thought (Todd and McKee 4-5).

11. These letters, held at the Public Record Office, are transcribed by Cameron (34-86). Goreau concisely summarizes and annotates them (90-112).

12. It is not known precisely how many plays Behn wrote, since several anonymous plays are attributed to her and several titles attributed to her have been lost; sixteen plays are extant.

13. After *The Forced Marriage, or The Jealous Bridegroom* the Dorset Garden Theatre produced *The Amorous Prince, or The Curious Husband* (1671); *The Dutch Lover* (1673); *The Town Fop, or Sir Timothy Tawdry* (1676); and *Abdelazer, or The Moor's Revenge*, a tragedy (1676). Two anonymous plays of 1677 have been attributed to Behn, *The Debauchee, or The Credulous Cuckold* and *The Counterfeit Bridegroom, or The Defeated Widow* (Stanton 340-41).

14. For a brief survey of unfavourable opinions of Behn's "immoral" subject matter see Hutner ("Introduction" to *Rereading* 2).

15. Playwrights were paid the proceeds from the third day's performance of a play.

16. Two of Katherine Philips' heroic dramas were produced in the 1660s, and Francis Boothby and Elizabeth Polwhele each had one play produced, but none of the three defined herself as a professional writer.

17. Nicoll notes with surprise that Mary Sanderson, the actress who married the actor Thomas Betterton, had no scandal attached to her name (71). The Sanderson/Betterton marriage prefigures the many professional and marital partnerships which characterized the British theatre in the eighteenth and nineteenth centuries, including those of the Garricks, Siddons, Kembles, and Keans.

18. A case in point is an actress named Rebecca Marshall, who was kidnapped by a courtier in spite of appealing to the king for protection (Howe 33; Goreau 160).

19. However, not all crossdressing disappeared; male actors continue to caricature older women in what are now known as "dame parts."

20. Many of Shakespeare's plays were revised between 1660 and 1690; the works of Beaumont and Fletcher, and of Thomas Middleton, as well as other playwrights, were also favourite sources for adaptations in the late seventeenth century.

21. Behn's prose works are more innovative in terms of genre than her plays. In particular *Oroonoko* and *Love Letters* are by many critics seen as prescient precursors of the novel. See, for example, Janet Todd's discussion in *The Sign of Angellica* (76-83).

22. Behn's ambiguous reference to Brome in the "Postscript" may be designed to suggest that Killigrew also drew on Brome. For Killigrew's sources, see Alfred Harbage (119-222), who briefly discusses Killigrew's debts to Calderón's *La Dama Duende* (180, n. 4; 221) as well as to John Fletcher's *The Captain* and Ben Jonson's *Volpone* (221-22). Harbage also discusses autobiographical elements in *Thomaso* (102; 106-7;116).

23. See Harold Weber's discussion of Thomaso as rake and Angellica as female libertine (153-61).

24. For a general analysis of Behn's revision of Killigrew see Jones DeRitter. Nancy Copeland focusses on Behn's treatment of Killigrew's women characters ("Once a Whore"). See also Heidi Hutner's interesting discussion of "the resistance of the 'other' body" in both parts of *The Rover*.

25. The rake's place in Restoration drama of this period is discussed in detail by Harold Weber.

26. Mark Lussier briefly sketches some of the ways in which theoretical discussion of the carnivalesque might be applied to *The Rover* ("Marrying" 231-32); see Terry Castle for a more developed theoretical framework of the carnivalesque in Restoration and eighteenth-century literature.

27. The importance of the mask is central to most discussions of Restoration drama. For a brief outline of the function of the mask see Bevis (71-72). For a description of masquerade costumes and an analysis of the importance of the masquerade in eighteenth-century society, see Terry Castle, *Masquerade and Civilization* (chapters 1 and 2).

28. Lussier develops Diamond's argument when he suggests that "women are consumable commodities who circulate within a masculine economy of desire" ("Marrying" 234). See also Lussier's discussion of Behn's use of economic language in her later plays *The City Heiress* and *The Feigned Courtesans* ("Vile Merchandize").

29. Discussions of the frequency of rape as a plot motif in Restoration drama tend to focus on tragedy and heroic drama. See Susan Staves' discussion of rape as property crime in heroic drama (59, 259) and Jean I. Marsden on the relation of rape and chastity in Restoration adaptations of Shakespeare (52-54). Elizabeth Howe discusses Restoration rape scenes as "voyeurism" (43-49).

30. *The Rover* is not the only play in which Behn employs conventional antisemitic stereotypes; in *The Second Part of the Rover* two women characters named in the *Dramatis Personae* as a monster and a dwarf are described to Willmore as "two Jewish Monsters arriv'd from Mexico, Jews of vast Fortunes, with an old Jew Uncle their Guardian" (Summers, *Works of Aphra Behn* 1: 124).

31. Willmore takes gold from Angellica, though he returns it when she threatens him with a pistol. At the beginning of *The Second*

Part of The Rover he notes that Hellena died after a few months of marriage, and that her large dowry is already spent.

32. Seventeenth-century audiences seem to have consistently focused on Willmore and Blunt as favourite characters. Hellena dies before the opening of the sequel, in which Willmore's drinking, sexual adventures and complicated intrigues are the centre of the plot.

33. Hutner argues that patriarchal authority, which is restored at the end of the first part of *The Rover*, is undercut in the sequel ("Revisioning" *passim*).

34. Genest asserts that Nell Gwyn acted at Dorset Garden Theatre, (1:210); other sources, including the *Dictionary of National Biography*, also indicate that Nell Gwyn played Angellica Bianca. For a discussion of the confusion between Anne Quin and Nell Gwyn see *A Biographical Dictionary of London Actors* (12:244).

35. Nancy Cotton argues that in *The Rover* Angellica Bianca "loses" Willmore to Hellena because she is "humourless" (*Women Playwrights* 65); but that La Nuche in *The Second Part of the Rover* is able to "win" Willmore because she "has the wit and sense of humour that Angellica Bianca lacked" (*Women Playwrights* 67). In assessing the trajectory of Behn's comedies at this point in her career, Cotton suggests that "In each case, the more generous woman gets the man" (*Women Playwrights* 67). See also Heidi Hutner's analysis of the two parts of *The Rover* in relation to Killigrew's *Thomaso*.

36. Unidentified clipping of 9 March 1790, in file on *Love in Many Masks* held at Covent Garden Theatre Museum Library.

37. The play has also been produced by the Revels Players at the University of Illinois, Champaign-Urbana, April 1990 (rev. *Daily Illini* 18 April, 1990), at the Union Theatre in Peterborough, Ontario, February 1-6, 1994; at the Jacob Street Film Studios, London, in November 1994; and at the Guthrie Theatre, Minneapolis in the summer of 1995.

Selected Bibliography

References to secondary sources cited in the "Introduction" are listed under "Sources," as are some other useful works relating to Behn. Adaptations of *The Rover*, some recent editions of *The Rover*, and other works by Behn are listed under the heading "Adaptations and Modern Editions of Behn's Works."

Early editions of *The Rover* which I have consulted for this edition are briefly described in "A Note on the Text," and are listed at the beginning of the "Textual Notes" immediately following the play.

Modern Editions and Adaptations of Behn's Works

Behn, Aphra. *An Adaptation of The Rover: A Programme/Text With Commentary by Simon Trussler*. Swan Theatre Plays. London: Methuen with Royal Shakespeare Company, [1987].

_____. *Five Plays: The Lucky Chance, The Rover Part 1, The Widow Ranter, The False Count, Abdelazer*. Introduced by Maureen Duffy. London: Methuen, 1990.

_____. *Oroonoko, or The Royal Slave*. Ed. Adelaide P. Amore. Lanham, MD: University Press of America, 1987.

_____. *Oroonoko, The Rover and Other Works*. Ed. Janet Todd. Harmondsworth: Penguin, 1992: 155-248.

_____. *The Rover*. Ed. Frederick M. Link. Regent's Restoration Drama Series. Lincoln: University of Nebraska Press, 1967.

_____. *The Rover*. The HBJ Anthology of Drama. Ed. W.B. Worthen. Fort Worth: Harcourt Brace Jovanovich, 1993: 321-53

_____. *The Works of Aphra Behn*. Ed. Janet Todd. 7 vols. Columbus: Ohio State University Press, 1992-6.

_____. *The Rover*. Vol. 2 of *Restoration Comedy*. Ed. A. Norman Jeffares. 4 vols. London: Folio Press, 1974: 230-331.

_____. *The Works of Aphra Behn*. Ed Montague Summers. 6 vols. London: 1915. New York: Phaeton, 1967.

_____. *The Uncollected Verse of Aphra Behn.* Ed. Germaine Greer. Stump Cross, Essex: Stump Cross, 1989.

Kemble, J.P. *Love in Many Masks.* London, 1790.

Sources

Agate, James, ed. *The English Dramatic Critics, An Anthology: 1660-1932.* London: Arthur Barker, [1932].

Armistead, J.M. *Four Restoration Playwrights: A Reference Guide to Thomas Shadwell, Aphra Behn, Nathaniel Lee, and Thomas Otway.* Boston: G.K. Hall, 1984.

Bassett, Kate. "A-roving." Rev. of *The Rover,* Jacob Street Film Studios, London. *Times Literary Supplement* 4781 (18 November, 1994): 18.

Bevis, Richard W. *English Drama: Restoration and Eighteenth Century, 1660-1789.* London and New York: Longman, 1988.

A Biographical Dictionary of Actors, Actresses, Musicians, Dancers, Managers and Other Stage Personnel in London, 1660-1800. Ed. Philip H. Highfill Jr., Kalman A. Burnim and Edward A. Langhans. 16 vols. Carbondale and Edwardsville: Southern Illinois University Press, 1973-93.

Brown, Laura. *English Dramatic Form, 1660-1760: An Essay in Generic History.* New Haven and London: Yale University Press, 1981.

Burns, Edward. *Restoration Comedy: Crises of Desire and Identity.* New York: St. Martin's Press, 1987.

Cameron, W.J. *New Light on Aphra Behn.* Auckland: University of Auckland Press, 1961.

Campbell, Elaine. "Aphra Behn's Surinam Interlude." *Kunapipi* 7.2-3 (1985): 25-35.

Carlson, Susan. *Women and Comedy: Rewriting the British Theatrical Tradition.* Ann Arbor: University of Michigan Press, 1991.

_____. "Cannibalizing and Carnivalizing: Reviving Aphra Behn's *The Rover.*" *Theatre Journal* 47.4 (December 1995): 517-39.

Castle, Terry. *Masquerade and Civilization: The Carnivalesque in Eighteenth-Century English Culture and Fiction.* Stanford: Stanford University Press, 1986.

Caywood, Cynthia L. and Bonnie A. Hain. "Cutting the Gordian Knot: The Humor of Aphra Behn and Roseanne Arnold." *Restoration and 18th Century Theatre Research* second series, 9.2 (Winter 1994): 45-65.

Copeland, Nancy. "'Once a whore and ever'? Whore and Virgin in *The Rover* and its Antecedents." *Restoration* 16.1 (Spring 1992): 20-27.

_____. "Reproducing *The Rover*: John Barton's *Rover* at the Swan." *Essays in Theatre* 9.1 (Nov. 1990): 45-59.

Cotton, Nancy. "Aphra Behn and the Pattern Hero." *Curtain Calls: British and American Women and the Theatre, 1660-1820.* Ed. Mary Anne Schofield and Cecilia Macheski. Athens: Ohio University Press, 1991. 211-19.

_____. *Women Playwrights in England c. 1363-1750.* Lewisburg: Bucknell University Press; London and Toronto: Associated University Presses, 1980.

Day, Robert Adams. "Aphra Behn's First Biography." *Studies in Bibliography* 22 (1969): 227-40.

DeRitter, Jones. "The Gypsy, *The Rover,* and the Wanderer: Aphra Behn's Revision of Thomas Killigrew." *Restoration* 10.2 (Fall 1986): 82-92.

Diamond, Elin. "Gestus and Signature in *The Rover.*" *ELH* 56.3 (Fall 1989): 519-41.

Duffy, Maureen. *The Passionate Shepherdess: Aphra Behn 1640-89.* London: Jonathan Cape, 1977.

Ferris, Lesley. *Acting Women: Images of Women in Theatre.* New York: New York University Press, 1989.

Fitzmaurice, James. "Aphra Behn and the *Abraham's Sacrifice Case.*" *Huntington Library Quarterly* 56 (Summer 1993): 319-27.

Franseschina, John. "Shadow and Substance in Aphra Behn's *The Rover*: The Semiotics of Restoration Performance." *Restoration* 19.1 (Spring 1995): 29-42.

Gallagher, Catherine. "Who Was That Masked Woman? The Prostitute and the Playwright in the Comedies of Aphra Behn." *Rereading Aphra Behn: History, Theory, and Criticism.* Ed. Heidi Hutner. Charlottesville and London: University Press of Virginia, 1993: 65-85. Previously published in *Women's Studies* 15 (1988): 77-83, and in *Last Laughs: Perspectives on Women and Comedy.* Ed. Regina Barreca. New York: Gordon and Breach, 1988.

Gardiner, Judith Kegan. "Aphra Behn: Sexuality and Self-respect." *Women's Studies* 7 (1980): 67-78.

Genest, John. *Some Account of the English Stage, From the Restoration in 1660 to 1830.* 10 vols. 1832. New York: Burt Franklin, [1965].

Gill, Pat. *Interpreting Ladies: Women, Wit and Morality in the Restoration Comedy of Manners.* Athens and London: University of Georgia Press, 1994.

Goreau, Angeline. *Reconstructing Aphra: A Social Biography of Aphra Behn.* New York: Dial, 1980.

Gussow, Mel. "Stage: *The Rover*, of 17th Century," Review of *The Rover* by Aphra Behn. Folger Theatre Group, Washington. *New York Times*, 14 January, 1982: C17.

Harbage, Alfred. *Thomas Killigrew, Cavalier Dramatist 1612-83*. 1930. New York: Benjamin Blom, 1967.

Hargreaves, H.A. "A Case for Mr. Behn." *Notes and Queries* June 1962: 203-205.

_____. "Mrs. Behn's Warning of the Dutch 'Thames Plot'." *Notes & Queries* February 1962: 61-63.

Hobby, Elaine. *English Women's Writing 1646-1688*. London: Virago, 1988.

Holland, Peter. *The Ornament of Action: Text and Performance in Restoration Comedy*. Cambridge: Cambridge University Press, 1979.

Hopkins, P.A. "Aphra Behn and John Hoyle: A Contemporary Mention, and Sir Charles Sedley's Poem on his Death." *Notes & Queries* ns. 42.2: 176-85.

Hornby, Richard. "The Guthrie Theatre." Rev. of *The Rover*. *Hudson Review* 47 (Winter 1995): 609-15.

Howe, Elizabeth. *The First English Actresses: Women and Drama 1660-1700*. Cambridge: Cambridge University Press, 1992.

Hume, Robert D. Rev. of *The Rover*. University of Illinois, Chicago Circle. *Theatre Journal* 31.3 (Oct. 1979): 412-13.

Hurren, Kenneth. "*The Rover*." Rev. of *The Rover*, The Swan, Stratford. *Plays and Players* 396 (Sept. 1988): 24-25.

Hutner, Heidi, ed. *Rereading Aphra Benn: History, Theory and Criticism*. Charlottesville: University Press of Virginia, 1993.

_____. "Revisioning the Female Body: Aphra Behn's *The Rover* Parts I and II" in *Rereading Aphra Behn: History, Theory, and Criticism*. Ed. Heidi Hutner. Charlottesville and London: University Press of Virginia, 1993. 102-20.

Jacobs, Naomi. "The Seduction of Aphra Behn." *Women's Studies* 18:4 (Jan. 1991): 379-93.

Jerrold, Walter, and Clare Jerrold. "Aphra Behn: The Incomparable Astraea" in *Five Queer Women*. London: Brentano's, 1929. 1-82.

Jones, Jane. "New Light on the Background and Early Life of Aphra Behn." *Notes and Queries* ns. 37:3 (Sept. 1990): 288-292. Reprinted in *Aphra Behn Studies*. Ed. Janet Todd. Cambridge: Cambridge University Press, 1996. 310-20.

Kavenik, Frances M. "Aphra Behn: the Playwright as 'Breeches Part'." *Curtain Calls: British and American Women and the Theatre, 1660-1820*. Ed. Mary Anne Schofield and Cecilia Macheski. Athens: Ohio University Press, 1991. 177-92.

Killigrew, Thomas. *Thomaso, or The Wanderer. Comedies and Tragedies*. London: 1664.

Langbaine, Gerard. *An Account of the English Dramatick Poets*. 1691. 2 vols. Los Angeles: William Andrews Clark Memorial Library, University of California, 1971.

Langdell, Cheri Davis. "Aphra Behn and Sexual Politics: A Dramatist's Discourse With Her Audience." *Drama, Sex and Politics*. Ed. James Redmond. *Themes in Drama*. Cambridge: Cambridge University Press, 1985. 109-28.

Langhans, Edward A. "Three Early Eighteenth-Century Promptbooks." *Theatre Notebook* 20 (Summer 1966): 142-50.

_____. "Tough Actresses to Follow." *Curtain Calls: British and American Women and the Theatre, 1660-1820*. Ed. Mary Anne Schofield and Cecilia Macheski. Athens: Ohio University Press, 1991. 3-17.

Link, Frederick M. *Aphra Behn*. New York: Twayne, 1968.

The London Stage 1660-1800: A Calendar of Plays, Entertainments & Afterpieces Together with Casts, Box-receipts and Contemporary Comment Compiled from the Playbills, Newspapers and Theatrical Diaries of the Period. Part 1, 1660-1700. Ed. William van Lennep. Carbondale: University of Illinois Press, 1960.

Lussier, Mark. "'Marrying that Hated Object': The Carnival of Desire in Behn's *The Rover*." *Privileging Gender in Early Modern England*. Ed Jean R. Brink. *Sixteenth-Century Essays & Studies*, Vol. XXIII. Kirksville, Missouri: Sixteenth Century Journal Publishers, 1993: 225-39.

_____. "'The Vile Merchandize of Fortune': Women, Economy and Desire in Aphra Behn." *Women's Studies* 18 (1991): 379-93.

Markley, Robert. "'Be impudent, be saucy, forward, bold, touzing and leud:' The Politics of Masculine Sexuality and Feminine Desire in Behn's Tory Comedies." *Cultural Readings of Restoration and Eighteenth-Century English Theater*, ed J. Douglas Canfield and Deborah C. Payne. Athens and London: University of Georgia Press, 1995. 114-40.

Marsden, Jean I. "Rewritten Women: Shakespearean Heroines in the Restoration." *The Appropriation of Shakespeare: Post-Renaissance Reconstructions of the Work and the Myth*. Ed. Jean I. Marsden. New York: St. Martin's, 1991. 43-56.

Medoff, Jeslyn. "The Daughters of Behn and the Problem of Reputation." *Women, Writing, History 1640-1740*. Ed. Isobel Grundy and Susan Wiseman. Athens: University of Georgia Press, 1992. 33-54.

Mendelson, Sara Heller. "Aphra Behn." *The Mental World of Stuart Women: Three Studies*. Brighton: Harvester, 1987. 116-84.

Munns, Jessica, "Barton and Behn's *The Rover*: or, The Text Transpos'd." *Restoration and Eighteenth Century Theatre Research*, 2nd series 3.2 (Winter 1988): 11-22.

_____. "'Good, Sweet, Honey, Sugar-Candied Reader': Aphra Behn's Foreplay in Forewords." *Rereading Aphra Behn: History, Theory, and Criticism.* Ed. Heidi Hutner. Charlottesville and London: University Press of Virginia, 1993. 44-64.

_____. "'I By A Double Right Thy Bounties Claim': Aphra Behn and Sexual Space." *Curtain Calls: British and American Women and the Theater, 1660-1820.* Ed. Mary Ann Schofield and Cecilia Macheski. Athens: Ohio University Press, 1991. 193-210.

Musser, Joseph F. Jr., "'Imposing Nought but Constancy in Love:' Aphra Behn Snares *The Rover*." *Restoration* 3.1 (Spring 1979): 17-25.

Nicoll, Allardyce. *Restoration Drama 1660-1700.* Vol. 1 of *A History of English Drama 1660-1900.* 6 vols. 4th ed. Cambridge: Cambridge University Press, 1955.

O'Donnell, Mary Ann. *Aphra Behn: An Annotated Bibliography of Primary and Secondary Sources.* New York: Garland, 1986.

Payne, Deborah C. "'And Poets Shall by Patron-Princes Live': Aphra Behn and Patronage." *Curtain Calls: British and American Women and the Theater, 1660-1820.* Ed. Mary Ann Schofield and Cecilia Macheski. Athens: Ohio University Press, 1991. 105-19.

Pearson, Jacqueline. *The Prostituted Muse: Images of Women and Women Dramatists 1642-1737.* New York: St. Martin's, 1988.

Platt, Harrison Gray Jr. "Astrea and Celadon: An Untouched Portrait of Aphra Behn." *PMLA* 49 (1934): 544-59.

Rich, Frank. "Stage: *The Rover*, Feminist Comedy From 1677." Review of *The Rover* by Aphra Behn. Williamstown Theater Festival, Williamstown. *New York Times*, July 27, 1987: C18.

Sackville-West, V. *Aphra Behn: The Incomparable Astrea.* New York: Viking, 1928.

Salvaggio, Ruth. "Aphra Behn's Love: Fiction, Letters and Desire." *Rereading Aphra Behn: History, Theory, and Criticism.* Ed. Heidi Hutner. Charlottesville and London: University Press of Virginia, 1993. 253-72.

Schofield, Mary Ann, and Cecilia Macheski, eds. *Curtain Calls: British and American Women and the Theater, 1660-1820.* Athens, Ohio University Press, 1991.

Scouten, Arthur H., and Robert D. Hume "'Restoration Comedy' and its Audience." *The Rakish Stage: Studies in English Drama.* Ed. Robert D.

Hume. Carbondale and Edwardsville: Illinois University Press, 1983. 46-81.

Shulman, Jeff. "An Ovidian Echo in Behn's *The Rover*." *Notes & Queries* 311 (Sept. 1984): 345-46.

Southerne, Thomas. *Oroonoko*. Ed. Maximilian E. Novak and David Stuart Ross. Lincoln: University of Nebraska Press, 1976.

Spencer, Jane. "*The Rover* and the Eighteenth Century." *Aphra Behn Studies*. Ed. Janet Todd. Cambridge: Cambridge University Press, 1996. 84-106.

Stanton, Judith Philips. "'This New-Found Path Attempting': Serious Plays by Women on the London Stage 1660-1737." *Curtain Calls: British and American Women and the Theater, 1660-1820*. Ed. Mary Ann Schofield and Cecilia Macheski. Athens: Ohio University Press, 1991. 325-56.

Staves, Susan. *Players' Sceptres: Fictions of Authority in the Restoration*. Lincoln and London: University of Nebraska Press, 1979.

Stiebel, Arlene. "Not Since Sappho: The Erotic in Poems of Katherine Philips and Aphra Behn." *Homosexuality in Renaissance and Enlightenment England: Literary Representations in Historical Context*. Ed. Claude Summers. Binghamton, NY: Harrington Park Press; New York: Haworth, 1992. 153-71.

Sullivan, David M. "The Female Will in Aphra Behn." *Women's Studies* 22.3 (1993): 35-47.

Summers, Montague. *The Restoration Theatre*. London: Kegan Paul, Trench, Trubner & Co., 1934.

Todd, Janet. *The Sign of Angellica: Women, Writing and Fiction, 1660-1800*. London: Virago, 1989.

_____. *The Secret Life of Aphra Behn*. London: Andre Deutsch, 1996.

Todd, Janet, and Francis McKee. "The 'Shee Spy'; Unpublished letters on Aphra Behn, Secret Agent." *Times Literary Supplement*, 10 September, 1993: 4-5.

Ward, Charles E. *The Letters of John Dryden With Letters Addressed to Him*. 1942. New York: AMS, 1965.

Weber, Harold. *The Restoration Rake-Hero: Transformations in Sexual Understanding in Seventeenth-Century England*. Madison: University of Wisconsin Press, 1986.

Williamson, Marilyn. *Raising Their Voices: British Women Writers, 1650-1750*. Detroit: Wayne State University Press, 1990.

Wiseman, S.J. *Aphra Behn*. Plymouth: Northcote House, in association with the British Council, 1996.

Woodcock, George. *Aphra Behn: The English Sappho*. Montreal: Black Rose, 1989. Prev. pub. as *The Incomparable Aphra*. London: Boardman, 1948.

A Note on the Text

The first edition of *The Rover* was a quarto published in 1677, the year the play was first produced. The second edition was also published in quarto in 1697. The play appears in collected editions of Behn's works published in 1702 and 1724; a third quarto was published in 1709. The copytext for this edition of *The Rover* is the first edition of 1677, which is coherent and includes many detailed stage directions; it exists in three issues, described in detail by Mary Ann O'Donnell (32-38); see also Frederick Link (*Rover* ix-x). These three issues are illuminating for what they tell us about Behn's acknowledgment of authorship. Although the title pages of the first two issues do not name the author, the "Prologue" of all three issues refers to the author as "he". The third issue, however, adds "written by Mrs. A. Behn" to the title page. In some copies of the second issue, and in the third issue the author's "Postscript" is printed with the addition of the phrase "especially of our sex", an acknowledgment that the author is a woman.

I have collated copies of the first edition held by the British Library and the Thomas Fisher Rare Book Library at the University of Toronto with a microfilm of the Huntington Library copy. In addition, I have collated the British Library copies of the second and third quartos, and of the first two collected editions. In a few instances I have adopted readings from editions other than the first. These cases are indicated in the Textual Notes following the play. I have also consulted editions of *The Rover* by Montague Summers (1915), Frederick Link (1967), Norman Jeffares (1974) and Janet Todd (1992).

Spelling and capitalization have been modernized, and the many typefaces used in early editions, such as italic type for proper names within speeches, have been simplified. Long "s" is printed as "s"; ampersands are expanded to "and". When a contraction in the 1677 text has no effect on pronunciation, as when "'d" represents a silent "ed" ending, modern spelling is used. (For example, "shock'd" is changed to "shocked".) However, when a contraction suggests pronunciation, I have preserved its spelling, as, for example, "'twill" for "it will", "for't" for "for it", "e'er" for "ever", "'tis" for "it is", etc. When different spellings of a word are used in the first edition, I have regularized them. In the 1677 edition, for example, "pistol" and "pistole" are used interchangeably to signify either a gun or a coin; I use "pistol" for the gun, and "pistole" for the coin. The regularized form "'sheartlikins" is used for the variants "sheartlikins", "'dsheartlikins", "adsheartlikins" and "adshartlikins" which appear in the 1677 edition. As well, I have retained a few non-standard spellings which suggest pronunciation, such as "learnt" for "learned". In a few cases spelling in the 1677 edition is ambiguous; I have recorded the variants in the Textual Notes.

Although most of *The Rover* is written in prose, the play includes a few songs and verses. There are also some sententious or sentimental speeches which in the early editions have been set as poetry, and which are often metrically irregular. I have retained these passages as poetry. Textual notes are indicated by a dagger (†).

The first edition of *The Rover* includes detailed stage directions. A double-dagger (‡) indicates stage directions I have added.

As much as possible, I have retained the punctuation of the 1677 edition. The many dashes, run-on sentences and sentence fragments evoke energetic, colloquial speech, suggesting how lines might have been delivered on the seventeenth-century stage. While I have punctuated some extremely long sentences with semi-colons and full stops, my aim has been been to alter the rhythms of the speeches as little as possible.

THE ROVER

PROLOGUE

Wits, like physicians, never can agree,
When of a different society.
And Rabel's Drops were never more cried down
By all the learned doctors of the town,
Than a new play whose author is unknown.　　　　　5
Nor can those doctors with more malice sue
(And powerful purses) the dissenting few,
Than those with an insulting price do rail
At all who are not of their own cabal.
　　If a young poet hit your humour right,　　　　10
You judge him then out of revenge and spite.
So amongst men there are ridiculous elves,
Who monkeys hate for being too like themselves.
So that the reason of the grand debate,
Why wit so oft is damned, when good plays take,　　15
Is that you censure as you love, or hate.
　　Thus like a learned conclave poets sit,
Catholic. judges both of sense and wit,
And damn or save, as they themselves think fit.
Yet those who to others' faults are so severe,　　20
Are not so perfect but themselves may err.
Some write correct[†] *indeed, but then the whole*
(Bating their own dull stuff i'th' play) is stole;
As bees do suck from flowers their honey dew,
So they rob others striving to please you.　　　　25
　　Some write their characters gentle[†] *and fine,*
But then they do so toil for every line,
That what to you does easy seem, and plain,
Is the hard issue of their labouring brain.
And some th'effects of all their pains we see,　　30
Is but to mimic good extempore.
Others by long converse about the town,

---

3 Rabel's Drops] a patent medicine
9 cabal] clique
17 conclave] meeting to elect a pope; private meeting
18 catholic] universal; broadminded

Have wit enough to write a lewd lampoon,
But their chief skill lies in a bawdy song.
In short, the only wit that's now in fashion,
Is but the gleanings of good conversation.
As for the author of this coming play,
I asked him   what he thought fit I should say
In thanks for your good company today:
He called me fool, and said it was well known
You came not here for our sakes, but your own.
New plays are stuffed with wits, and with debauches,[†]
That crowd and sweat like cits, in May-Day coaches.

Written by a Person of Quality..

---

38 him] the first edition of *The Rover* was published anonymously; the writer of the
   "Prologue" here speaks as if the author is a man. See "Introduction" for a discussion
   of Behn's situation as a woman writer and her acknowledgement of authorship.
43 cits] citizens; a derogatory term used by the leisured classes to refer to merchants and
   tradespeople concentrated in the City of London
43 May-Day coaches] It was the custom to ride around Hyde Park in coaches on May Day;
   possibly an urban variation on traditional May Day expeditions to the countryside.
44 Person of Quality] Prologues and Epilogues of Restoration plays were often
   contributed by someone other than the author of the play.

THE ACTORS' NAMES.

Mr. Jevon[†]	Don Antonio,	The Viceroy's son.
Mr. Medbourne[†]	Don Pedro,	A noble Spaniard, his friend.
Mr. Betterton	Belvile,	An English colonel in love with Florinda.
Mr. Smith	Willmore,	The ROVER.
Mr. Crosby[†]	Frederick,	An English gentleman and friend to Belvile and Blunt.[†]
Mr. Underhill	Blunt,	An English country gentle-man.
Mr. Richards	Stephano,	Servant to Don Pedro.
Mr. Percival[†]	Phillippo,	Lucetta's gallant.
Mr. John Lee	Sancho,	Pimp to Lucetta.
	Biskey, and Sebastian,	Two bravoes to Angellica.
	Officers and Soldiers.	
	Diego[‡] Page To Don Antonio.	
	Boy	

5 Rover] wanderer; also pirate
13 bravoes] hired soldiers; bodyguards

Women.

Mrs. Betterton	Florinda,	Sister to Don Pedro.
Mrs. Barry[†]	Hellena,	A gay young woman designed for a nun, and sister to Florinda.
Mrs. Hughes	Valeria,	A kinswoman to Florinda.
Mrs. Quin[†]	Angellica Bianca,	A famous courtesan.
Mrs. Leigh	Moretta,	Her woman.
Mrs. Norris	Callis,	Governess to Florinda and Hellena.
Mrs. Gillow[†]	Lucetta,	A jilting wench.
	Servants,	
	Other Masqueraders,	
	Men and Women.	

The Scene: NAPLES, in Carnival time.

---

34 Naples] Although the play is set in Naples, numerous traces of the the Spanish setting
  of *Thomaso* (Behn's source) remain in *The Rover*.
34 Carnival] pre-Lenten festival in which people wear costumes

The

ROVER

OR, The Banished Cavaliers.

ACT the First.
Scene the First. A Chamber.

Enter Florinda and Hellena.

FLORINDA.

What an impertinent thing is a young girl bred in a nunnery!   1
How full of questions! Prithee no more Hellena; I have told thee
more than thou understand'st already.

HELLENA.

The more's my grief. I would fain know as much as you, which
makes me so inquisitive; nor is't enough I know you're a lover,   5
unless you tell me too, who 'tis you sigh for.

FLORINDA.

When you're a lover, I'll think you fit for a secret of that nature.

HELLENA.

'Tis true, I never was a lover yet — but I begin to have a shrewd
guess what it is to be so, and fancy it very pretty to sigh, and sing,
and blush, and wish, and dream, and wish, and long and wish to   10
see the man, and when I do, look pale and tremble; just as you
did when my brother brought home the fine English colonel to
see you — what do you call him, Don Belvile?

Title: Cavaliers] Supporters of the English monarchy during the English civil war period.
Many cavaliers left England after the execution of King Charles I in 1649.

FLORINDA

> Fie, Hellena.

HELLENA

> That blush betrays you — I am sure 'tis so — or is it Don Antonio the viceroy's son? Or perhaps the rich old Don Vincentio whom my father designs you for a husband? Why do you blush again?

FLORINDA

> With indignation, and how near soever my father thinks I am to marrying that hated object, I shall let him see I understand better what's due to my beauty, birth and fortune, and more to my soul, than to obey those unjust commands.

HELLENA

> Now hang me if I don't love thee for that dear disobedience. I love mischief strangely, as most of our sex do, who are come to love nothing else — but tell me dear Florinda, don't you love that fine Anglese? For I vow, next to loving him myself, 'twill please me most that you do so, for he is so gay and so handsome.

FLORINDA.

> Hellena, a maid designed for a nun ought not to be so curious in a discourse of love.

HELLENA

> And dost thou think that ever I'll be a nun? Or at least till I'm so old, I'm fit for nothing else — faith no, sister; and because I hope he has some mad companion or other that will spoil my devotion, nay I'm resolved to provide myself this carnival, if there be e'er a handsome proper fellow of my humour above ground, though I ask first.

FLORINDA

> Prithee be not so wild.

HELLENA

> Now you have provided yourself of a man, you take no care for poor me — prithee tell me, what dost thou see about me that is unfit for love — have I not a world of youth? A humour gay? A beauty passable? A vigour desirable? Well shaped? Clean limbed? Sweet breathed? And sense enough to know how all these ought to be employed to the best advantage? Yes, I do and will; therefore lay aside your hopes of my fortune by my being a devote,

---

25   Anglese] Englishman

and tell me how you came acquainted with this Belvile, for I perceive you knew him before he came to Naples.

FLORINDA

Yes, I knew him at the siege of Pamplona;[†] he was then a colonel   45
of French horse, who when the town was ransacked, nobly
treated my brother and myself, preserving us from all insolences;
and I must own (besides great obligations) I have I know not
what that pleads kindly for him about my heart, and will suffer
no other to enter — but see, my brother.   50

Enter Don Pedro, Stephano with a masquing habit, and Callis.

PEDRO

Good morrow sister — pray, when saw you your lover Don Vincentio?

FLORINDA

I know not, sir — Callis, when was he here? For I consider it so little, I know not when it was.

PEDRO

I have a command from my father here to tell you you ought not   55
to despise him, a man of so vast a fortune and such a passion for
you — Stephano, my things.

Puts on his masquing habit.

FLORINDA

A passion for me, 'tis more than e'er I saw, or he had a desire
should be known — I hate Vincentio, sir, and I would not have a
man so dear to me as my brother follow the ill customs of our   60
country, and make a slave of his sister — and sir, my father's will
I'm sure you may divert.

PEDRO

I know not how dear I am to you, but I wish only to be ranked in
your esteem equal with the English Colonel[†] Belvile — why do

---

42 devote] a nun or religious person
45 Pamplona] a fortified town in Navarre
Stage Direction: masquing habit] costume worn at carnival

you frown and blush? Is there any guilt belongs to the name of   6
that cavalier?

FLORINDA.

I'll not deny I value Belvile. When I was exposed to such dangers
as the licensed lust of common soldiers threatened, when rage
and conquest flew through the city — then Belvile, this criminal
for my sake, threw[†] himself into all dangers to save my honour,   7
and will you not allow him my esteem?

PEDRO.

Yes, pay him what you will in honour — but you must consider
Don Vincentio's fortune, and the jointure he'll make you.

FLORINDA.

Let him consider my youth, beauty and fortune, which ought not
to be thrown away on his age and jointure.   7

PEDRO.

'Tis true, he's not so young and fine a gentleman as that Belvile —
but what jewels will that cavalier present you with? Those of his
eyes and heart?

HELLENA.

And are not those better than any Don Vincentio has brought
from the Indies?   8

PEDRO.

Why, how now! Has your nunnery breeding taught you to understand the value of hearts and eyes?

HELLENA.

Better than to believe Vincentio's deserve value from any woman
— he may perhaps increase her bags, but not her family.

PEDRO.

This is fine — go — up to your devotion; you are not designed for   8
the conversation of lovers.

HELLENA.   [*Aside.*]

Nor saints yet a while,[†] I hope.

— Is't not enough you make a nun of me, but you must cast my
sister away too, exposing her to a worse confinement than a religious life?   9

---

73 jointure] part of a marriage settlement which provides for a wife's support after her
   husband's death
84 bags] wealth

PEDRO.

>The girl's mad — it is a confinement to be carried into the country, to an ancient villa belonging to the family of the Vincentios these five hundred years, and have no other prospect than that pleasing one of seeing all her own that meets her eyes — a fine air, large fields, and gardens where she may walk and gather flowers. 95

HELLENA.

>When, by moonlight? For I am sure she dares not encounter with the heat of the sun; that were a task only for Don Vincentio and his Indian breeding, who loves it in the dog days — and if these be her daily divertisements, what are those of the night? To lie in 100 a wide moth-eaten bed chamber, with furniture in fashion in the reign of King Sancho the First; the bed, that which his forefathers lived and died in.

PEDRO.

>Very well.

HELLENA.

>This apartment (new furbished and fitted out for the young wife) 105 he (out of freedom) makes his dressing room, and being a frugal and jealous coxcomb, instead of a valet to uncase his feeble carcass, he desires you to do that office — signs of favour I'll assure you, and such as you must not hope for, unless your woman be out of the way. 110

PEDRO.

>Have you done yet?

HELLENA.

>That honour being past, the giant stretches itself, yawns and sighs a belch or two, loud as a musket, throws himself into bed, and expects you in his foul sheets, and ere you can get yourself 115 undressed, calls you with a snore or two — and are not these fine blessings to a young lady?

PEDRO.

>Have you done yet?

---

99 Indian breeding] presumably Don Vincentio was born in the Indies
99 dog days] hottest days of summer
100 divertisements] diversions
105 new furbished] refurbished

HELLENA.

And this man you must kiss; nay you must kiss none but him, too — and nuzzle through his beard to find his lips. And this you must submit to for threescore years, and all for a jointure.

PEDRO.

For all your character of Don Vincentio, she is as like to marry him as she was before.

HELLENA.

Marry Don Vincentio! Hang me, such a wedlock would be worse than adultery with another man. I had rather see her in the Hotel de Dieu[†], to waste her youth there in vows and be a handmaid to lazars and cripples, than to lose it in such a marriage.

PEDRO.

You have considered, sister, that Belvile has no fortune to bring you to — banished his country, despised at home, and pitied abroad.

HELLENA.

What then? The viceroy's son is better than that old Sir Fifty. Don Vincentio! Don Indian! He thinks he's trading to Gambo still and would barter himself (that bell and bauble) for your youth and fortune.

PEDRO.

Callis, take her hence, and lock her up all this Carnival, and at Lent she shall begin her everlasting penance in a monastery.

HELLENA.

I care not; I had rather be a nun than be obliged to marry as you would have me, if I were designed for't.

PEDRO.

Do not fear the blessing of that choice — you shall be a nun.

HELLENA.

Shall I so? You may chance to be mistaken in my way of devotion — a nun! Yes, I am like to make a fine nun! I have an excellent humour for a grate..

---

125 Hotel de Dieu] hospital run by nuns for the care of the destitute and outcast
126 lazars] people with Hansen's diseases (leprosy); more generally, diseased people
131 Gambo] Gambia, on the coast of Africa
141 grate] bars in the door of a convent, marking the separation of the nun from the world

[*Aside.*] I'll have a saint of my own to pray to shortly, if I like any that dares venture on me.

PEDRO.

Callis, make it your business to watch this wild cat. As for you Florinda, I've only tried you all this while and urged my father's will; but mine is that you would love Antonio. He is brave and young, and all that can complete the happiness of a gallant maid. This absence of my father will give us opportunity to free you from Vincentio by marrying here, which you must do tomorrow. 145

FLORINDA.

Tomorrow! 150

PEDRO.

Tomorrow, or 'twill be too late — 'tis not my friendship to Antonio which makes me urge this, but love to thee and hatred to Vincentio — therefore, resolve upon tomorrow.

FLORINDA.

Sir, I shall strive to do as shall become your sister.

PEDRO.

I'll both believe and trust you. Adieu. 155

Exeunt Pedro and Stephano.

HELLENA.

As becomes his sister! That is to be as resolved your way, as he is his —

Hellena goes to Callis.

FLORINDA.

I ne'er till now perceived my ruin near.
I've no defence against Antonio's love,
For he has all the advantages of nature, 160
The moving arguments of youth and fortune.

HELLENA.

But hark you, Callis, you will not be so cruel to lock me up indeed, will you?

CALLIS.

I must obey the commands I have[†] — besides, do you consider what a life you are going to lead?

HELLENA.

Yes, Callis, that of a nun; and till then I'll be indebted a world of prayers to you if you'll let me now see what I never did, the divertisements of a carnival.

CALLIS.

What, go in masquerade? 'Twill be a fine farewell to the world, I take it — pray, what would you do there?

HELLENA.

That which all the world does, as I am told — be as mad as the rest and take all innocent freedoms. Sister, you'll go too, will you not? Come, prithee be not sad. We'll outwit twenty brothers if you'll be ruled by me — come, put off this dull humour with your clothes, and assume one as gay, and as fantastic, as the dress my cousin Valeria and I have provided, and let's ramble.

FLORINDA.

Callis, will you give us leave to go?

CALLIS. [*Aside.*]

I have a youthful itch of going myself. — Madam, if I thought your brother might not know it, and I might wait on you; for by my troth I'll not trust young girls alone.

FLORINDA.

Thou see'st my brother's gone already, and thou shalt attend, and watch us.

Enter Stephano.

STEPHANO.

Madam,[†] the habits are come, and your cousin Valeria is dressed, and stays for you.

FLORINDA.

'Tis well. I'll write a note, and if I chance to see Belvile, and want an opportunity to speak to him, that shall let him know what I've resolved in favour of him.

HELLENA.

Come, let's in and dress us.

Exeunt.

A Long Street

Enter Belvile melancholy, Blunt and Frederick.

FREDERICK.

Why[†] what the devil ails the colonel? In a time when all the world
is gay, to look like mere Lent thus? Had'st thou been long
enough in Naples to have been in love, I should have sworn some
such judgment had befallen thee.

BELVILE.

No, I have made no new amours since I came to Naples.   5

FREDERICK.

You have left none behind you in Paris?

BELVILE.

Neither.

FREDERICK.

I cannot divine the cause then, unless the old cause, the want of
money.

BLUNT.

And another old cause, the want of a wench — would not that re-   10
vive you?

BELVILE.

You are mistaken, Ned.

BLUNT.

Nay, 'sheartlikins, then thou'rt past cure.

FREDERICK.

I have found it out; thou hast renewed thy acquaintance with the
lady that cost thee so many sighs at the siege of Pamplona — pox   15
on't, what d'ye call her — her brother's a noble Spaniard —
nephew to the dead general — Florinda — ay Florinda — and will
nothing serve thy turn but that damned virtuous woman? Whom
on my conscience thou lovest in spite too, because thou seest little or no possibility of gaining her.   20

---

13 'sheartlikins] God's little heart; a "minced oath" combining "God's heart" and
"bodikin." Also "heartikin," "adsheartlikins."

BELVILE.

Thou art mistaken. I have interest enough in that lovely virgin's heart to make me proud and vain, were it not abated by the severity of a brother, who perceiving my happiness —

FREDERICK.

Has civilly forbid thee the house?

BELVILE.

'Tis so; to make way for a powerful rival, the viceroy's son, who has the advantage of me in being a man of fortune, a Spaniard, and her brother's friend; which gives him liberty to make his court, whilst I have recourse only to letters and distant looks from her window, which are as soft and kind as those which heaven sends down on penitents.

BLUNT.

Heyday! 'Sheartlikins, simile! By this light, the man is quite spoiled. Fred, what the devil are we made of that we cannot be thus concerned for a wench? 'Sheartlikins, our cupids are like the cooks of the camp, they can roast or boil a woman, but they have none of the fine tricks to set 'em off, no hogoes to make the sauce pleasant and the stomach sharp.

FREDERICK.

I dare swear I have had a hundred as young, kind and handsome as this Florinda; and dogs eat me, if they were not as troublesome to me i'the morning as they were welcome o'er night.

BLUNT.

And yet I warrant he would not touch another woman if he might have her for nothing.

BELVILE.

That's thy joy, a cheap whore.

BLUNT.

Why 'sheartlikins, I love a frank soul — when did you ever hear of an honest woman that took a man's money? I warrant 'em good ones — but gentlemen, you may be free, you have been kept so poor with Parliaments and Protectors, that the little stock you

---

35 hogoes] piquant or strongly-flavoured mixtures used in cooking; relishes

46 Protectors] During the period of Parliamentary rule, Oliver Cromwell used the title of Protector of England.

have is not worth preserving — but I thank my stars, I had more grace than to forfeit my estate by cavaliering.

BELVILE.

Methinks only following the court, should be sufficient to entitle 'em to that.   50

BLUNT.

'Sheartlikins, they know I follow it to do it no good, unless they pick a hole in my coat for lending you money now and then, which is a greater crime to my conscience, gentlemen, than to the Commonwealth.

Enter Willmore.

WILLMORE.

Ha! Dear Belvile! Noble colonel!   55

BELVILE.

Willmore! Welcome ashore, my dear rover! What happy wind blew us this good fortune?

WILLMORE.

Let me salute. my dear Frederick and then command me. How is't, honest lad?

FREDERICK.

Faith, sir, the old complement, infinitely the better to see my   60
dear mad Willmore again. Prithee, why camest thou ashore? And where's the Prince?

WILLMORE.

He's well, and reigns still lord of the watery element. I must aboard again within a day or two, and my business ashore was only to enjoy myself a little this carnival.   65

---

48 cavaliering] During the protectorate, cavaliers who left England could have their estates confiscated. Blunt boasts that he has managed to travel overseas without identifying himself, or being identified, as a cavalier, and hence is not liable to lose his property.

49 court] of the exiled Prince Charles, later Charles II

54 Commonwealth] name for England during Parliamentary rule

58 salute] kiss

62 Prince] Prince Charles

BELVILE.

Pray know our new friend, sir; he's but bashful, a raw traveller, but honest, stout and one of us.

Embraces Blunt.

WILLMORE.

That you esteem him gives him an interest here.

BLUNT.

Your servant, sir.

WILLMORE.

But well — faith, I'm glad to meet you again in a warm climate, where the kind sun has its god-like power still over the wine and women — love and mirth are my business in Naples, and if I mistake not the place, here's an excellent market for chapmen of my humour.

BELVILE.

See, here be those kind merchants of love you look for.

Enter several men in masquing habits, some playing on music, others dancing after; women dressed like courtesans, with papers pinned on their breasts, and baskets of flowers in their hands.

BLUNT.

'Sheartlikins, what have we here?

FREDERICK.

Now the game begins.

WILLMORE.

Fine pretty creatures! May a stranger have leave to look and love? What's here — [*Reads the papers.*] "Roses for every month"?

BLUNT.

"Roses for every month"? What means that?

BELVILE.

They are, or would have you think, they're courtesans, who here in Naples, are to be hired by the month.

---

73 chapmen] merchants

WILLMORE.

Kind and obliging to inform us — pray, where do these roses grow? I would fain plant some of 'em in a bed of mine.

WOMEN.

Beware such roses, sir.   85

WILLMORE.

A pox of fear; I'll be baked with thee between a pair of sheets, and that's thy proper still; so I might but strew such roses over me, and under me — fair one, would you would give me leave to gather at your bush this idle month; I would go near to make some body smell of it all the year after.   90

BELVILE.

And thou hast need of such a remedy, for thou stink'st of tar and rope's ends, like a dock or pest-house.

The woman puts herself into the hands of a man and exeunt.

WILLMORE.

Nay, nay, you shall not leave me so.

BELVILE.

By all means use no violence here.

WILLMORE.

Death! Just as I was going to be damnably in love, to have her led   95
off! I could pluck that rose out of his hand, and even kiss the bed the bush grew in.

FREDERICK.

No friend to love like a long voyage at sea.

BLUNT.

Except a nunnery, Frederick.

WILLMORE.

Death! But will they not be kind? Quickly be kind? Thou know'st   100
I'm no tame fighter, but a rampant lion of the forest.

---

86 baked...still] Willmore's *double entendre* refers to the process by which rose petals are distilled to make rosewater.

92 pest-house] hospital for plague victims

Advance from the farther end of the scenes two men dressed all over with horns of several sorts, making grimaces at one another, with papers pinned on their backs.

BELVILE.

    Oh the fantastical rogues, how they're dressed! 'Tis a satire against the whole sex.

WILLMORE.

    Is this a fruit that grows in this warm country?

BELVILE.

    Yes, 'tis pretty to see these Italians start, swell and stab at the   10
word "cuckold," and yet stumble at horns on every threshold.

WILLMORE.

    See what's on their back — [*Reads*] "Flowers of every night."
Ah, rogue! And more sweet than "Roses of every month"! This is a gardener of Adam's own breeding.

They dance.

BELVILE.

    What think you of those grave people? Is a wake in Essex half so   11•
mad or extravagant?

WILLMORE.

    I like their sober grave way; 'tis a kind of legal authorized fornication, where the men are not chid for't, nor the women despised, as amongst our dull English even the monsieurs want that part of good manners.   11

BELVILE.

    But here in Italy a monsieur is the humblest, best-bred gentleman — duels are so baffled by bravoes, that an age shows not one but between a Frenchman and a hangman, who is as much too hard for him on the piazza, as they are for a Dutchman on the New Bridge. — but see, another crew.   12•

Stage Direction: horns] sign of a cuckold

113 chid] chided

119 piazza] plaza or square

120 Dutchman on the New Bridge] a reference to the French defeat of the Dutch at Niuewerbrug in 1673.

Enter Florinda, Hellena and Valeria, dressed like gypsies; Callis and
Stephano; Lucetta, Phillipo and Sancho in masquerade.

HELLENA.

Sister, there's your Englishman, and with him a handsome
proper fellow — I'll to him, and instead of telling him his fortune,
try my own.

WILLMORE.

Gypsies, on my life — sure these will prattle if a man cross their
hands. 125

Goes to Hellena.

Dear, pretty (and I hope) young devil, will you tell an amorous
stranger what luck he's like to have?

HELLENA.

Have a care how you venture with me, sir, lest[†] I pick your
pocket, which will more vex your English humour than an Italian
fortune will please you. 130

WILLMORE.

How the devil cam'st thou to know my country and humour?

HELLENA.

The first I guess by a certain forward impudence, which does not
displease me at this time; and the loss of your money will vex you
because I hope you have but very little to lose.

WILLMORE.

Egad child, thou'rt i'th'right; it is so little, I dare not offer it thee 135
for a kindness — but cannot you divine what other things of more
value I have about me, that I would more willingly part with?

HELLENA.

Indeed no, that's the business of a witch, and I am but a gypsy
yet. Yet without looking in your hand, I have a parlous guess 'tis
some foolish heart you mean, an inconstant English heart, as lit- 140
tle worth stealing as your purse.

WILLMORE.

Nay, then thou dost deal with the devil, that's certain — thou hast
guessed as right as if thou had'st been one of that number it has

---

124 cross their hands] with silver; payment for telling a fortune

languished for. I find you'll be better acquainted with it, nor can
you take it in a better time; for I am come from the sea, child, 145
and Venus not being propitious to me in her own element, I
have a world of love in store — would you would be good-natured
and take some on't off my hands.

HELLENA.

Why — I could be inclined that way — but for a foolish vow I am
going to make — to die a maid. 150

WILLMORE.

Then thou art damned without redemption, and as I am a good
Christian, I ought in charity to divert so wicked a design — there-
fore prithee, dear creature, let me know quickly when and where
I shall begin to set a helping hand to so good a work.

HELLENA.

If you should prevail with my tender heart (as I begin to fear you 155
will, for you have horrible loving eyes) there will be difficulty in't,
that you'll hardly undergo for my sake.

WILLMORE.

Faith child, I have been bred in dangers, and wear a sword that
has been employed in a worse cause than for a handsome kind
woman — name the danger — let it be anything but a long siege — 160
and I'll undertake it.

HELLENA.

Can you storm?

WILLMORE.

Oh most furiously.

HELLENA.

What think you of a nunnery wall? For he that wins me must gain
that first. 165

WILLMORE.

A nun! Oh how I love thee for't! There's no sinner like a young
saint — nay, now there's no denying me, the old law had no curse
(to a woman) like dying a maid; witness Jepthah's daughter.

---

146 Venus...element] Venus, goddess of love, emerged from the sea.
167 old law] Old Testament law
168 Jephthah's daughter] Jephthah delayed the sacrifice of his virginal daughter for two
    months while she "bewailed her virginity"; see Judges 11: 30-40.

HELLENA.

A very good text this, if well handled, and I perceive, Father Captain, you would impose no severe penance on her who were inclined to console herself, before she took orders. 170

WILLMORE.

If she be young and handsome.

HELLENA.

Ay, there's it — but if she be not —

WILLMORE.

By this hand, child, I have an implicit faith, and dare venture on thee with all faults — besides, 'tis more meritorious to leave the 175 world when thou hast tasted and proved the pleasure on't. Then, 'twill be a virtue in thee, which now will be pure ignorance.

HELLENA.

I perceive, good Father Captain, you design only to make me fit for heaven — but if on the contrary, you should quite divert me from it and bring me back to the world again, I should have a 180 new man to seek, I find; and what a grief that will be — for when I begin, I fancy I shall love like anything. I never tried yet.

WILLMORE.

Egad and that's kind — prithee dear creature, give me credit for a heart, for faith I'm a very honest fellow. Oh, I long to come first to the banquet of love! And such a swinging appetite I bring — 185 oh, I'm impatient — thy lodging, sweetheart, thy lodging, or I'm a dead man!

HELLENA.

Why must we be either guilty of fornication or murder if we converse with you men — and is there no difference between leave to love me, and leave to lie with me? 190

WILLMORE.

Faith, child, they were made to go together.

LUCETTA.

Are you sure this is the man?

Pointing to Blunt.

---

171 to take orders] to take religious vows
185 swinging] forcible, immense; also "swingeing"

SANCHO.

    When did I mistake your game?

LUCETTA.

    This is a stranger, I know by his gazing; if he be brisk, he'll ven-   19*
ture to follow me, and then, if I understand my trade, he's mine.
He's English too, and they say that's a sort of good-natured loving people, and have generally so kind an opinion of themselves,
that a woman of any wit may flatter 'em into any sort of fool she
pleases.

            She often passes by Blunt and gazes on him;
            he struts and cocks, and walks and gazes on her.

BLUNT.

    'Tis so — she is taken — I have beauties which my false glass at   20*
home did not discover.

FLORINDA.

    This woman watches me so, I shall get no opportunity to discover
myself to him, and so miss the intent of my coming — but as I
was saying, sir — [*Looking in his hand*] by this line you should be a
lover.   20

BELVILE.

    I thought how right you guessed,[†] all men are in love, or pretend
to be so — come and let me go, I'm weary of this fooling.

               Walks away.

FLORINDA.

    I will not, till you have confessed whether the passion that you
have vowed Florinda be true or false.

    She holds him, he strives to get from her. He turns quick towards her.

BELVILE.

    Florinda!   21

FLORINDA.

    Softly.

---

200 glass] mirror

BELVILE.

Thou hast named one will fix me here for ever.

FLORINDA.

She'll be disappointed then, who expects you this night at the garden gate, and if you fail not, as — let me see the other hand — you will go near to do — she vows to die or make you happy. 215

Looks on Callis, who observes 'em.

BELVILE.

What canst thou mean?

FLORINDA.

That which I say — farewell.

Offers to go.

BELVILE.

Oh charming sybil, stay, complete that joy which as it is will turn into distraction! Where must I be? At the garden gate? I know it — at night you say? I'll sooner forfeit heaven than disobey. 220

Enter Don Pedro and other masquers, and pass over the stage.

CALLIS.

Madam, your brother's here.

FLORINDA.

Take this to instruct you farther.

Gives him a letter, and goes off.

FREDERICK.

Have a care, sir, what you promise; this may be a trap laid by her brother to ruin you.

BELVILE.

Do not disturb my happiness with doubts. 225

Opens the letter.

---

218 sybil] in Greek antiquity, one who can foretell the future

WILLMORE.

My dear pretty creature, a thousand blessings on thee! Still in this habit you say? And after dinner at this place?

HELLENA.

Yes, if you will swear to keep your heart, and not bestow it between this and that.

WILLMORE.

By all the little gods of love, I swear I'll leave it with you, and if 230 you run away with it, those deities of justice will revenge me.

Exeunt all the women.

FREDERICK.

Do you know the hand?

BELVILE.

'Tis Florinda's.

All blessings fall upon the virtuous maid.

FREDERICK.

Nay, no idolatry; a sober sacrifice I'll allow you. 235

BELVILE.

Oh friends, the welcomest news! The softest letter! Nay, you shall all see it! And could you now be serious, I might be made the happiest man the sun shines on!

WILLMORE.

The reason of this mighty joy?

BELVILE.

See how kindly she invites me to deliver her from the threatened 240 violence of her brother — will you not assist me?

WILLMORE.

I know not what thou mean'st, but I'll make one at any mischief where a woman's concerned — but she'll be grateful to us for the favour, will she not?

BELVILE.

How mean you? 245

WILLMORE.

How should I mean? Thou know'st there's but one way for a woman to oblige me.

BELVILE.

Do not profane — the maid is nicely virtuous.

WILLMORE.

Who, pox, then she's fit for nothing but a husband, let her e'en
go, colonel.   250

FREDERICK.

Peace, she's the colonel's mistress, sir.

WILLMORE.

Let her be the devil; if she be thy mistress, I'll serve her — name
the way.

BELVILE.

Read here this postscript.

Gives him a letter.

WILLMORE.   [*Reads.*]

"At ten at night — at the garden gate — of which, if I cannot get   255
the key, I will contrive a way over the wall — come attended with
a friend or two."
Kind heart, if we three cannot weave a string to let her down a
garden wall, 'twere pity but the hangman wove one for us all.

FREDERICK.

Let her alone for that. Your woman's wit, your fair kind woman,   260
will out-trick a broker or a Jew, and contrive like a Jesuit in
chains — but see, Ned Blunt is stolen out after the lure of a damsel.

Exeunt Blunt and Lucetta.

BELVILE.

So he'll scarce find his way home again, unless we get him cried
by the bellman in the market-place, and 'twould sound prettily —   265
a lost English boy of thirty.

FREDERICK.

I hope 'tis some common crafty sinner, one that will fit him; it
may be she'll sell him for Peru; the rogue's sturdy and would
work well in a mine; at least I hope she'll dress him for our

---

265 bellman] town crier
267 fit] serve him right; punish him fitly
268 Peru] known for its many mines using slave labour

mirth, cheat him of all, then have him well-favouredly hanged
and turned out naked at midnight.

WILLMORE.

Prithee, what humour is he of that you wish him so well?

BELVILE.

Why of an English elder brother's humour, educated in a nurs-
ery, with a maid to tend him till fifteen, and lies with his grand-
mother till he's of age; one that knows no pleasure beyond riding
to the next fair, or going up to London with his right worshipful
father in Parliament-time, wearing gay clothes, or making honourable love to his lady mother's laundry-maid; gets drunk at a
hunting-match, and ten to one then gives some proofs of his
prowess. A pox upon him, he's our banker and has all our cash
about him; and if he fail, we are all broke.

FREDERICK.

Oh let him alone for that matter, he's of a damned stingy quality;
that will secure our stock. I know not in what danger it were indeed if the jilt should pretend she's in love with him, for 'tis a
kind believing coxcomb; otherwise if he part with more than a
piece of eight — geld† him; for which offer he may chance to be
beaten, if she be a whore of the first rank.

BELVILE.

Nay, the rogue will not be easily beaten, he's stout enough. Perhaps if they talk beyond his capacity he may chance to exercise
his courage upon some of them, else I'm sure they'll find it as difficult to beat as to please him.

WILLMORE.

'Tis a lucky devil to light upon so kind a wench!

FREDERICK.

Thou had'st a great deal of talk with thy little gypsy; could'st thou
do no good upon her? For mine was hard-hearted.

WILLMORE.

Hang her, she was some damned honest person of quality, I'm
sure, she was so very free and witty. If her face be but answerable
to her wit and humour, I would be bound to constancy this
month to gain her — in the meantime, have you made no kind ac-

27

27

28

28

29

29

---

286 geld] castrate; with a play on gold(?)

quaintance since you came to town? You do not use to be honest
so long, gentlemen.   300

FREDERICK.

Faith, love has kept us honest; we have been all fired with a
beauty newly come to town, the famous Paduana, Angellica Bianca.

WILLMORE.

What, the mistress of the dead Spanish general?

BELVILE.

Yes, she's now the only adored beauty of all the youth in Naples, 305
who put on all their charms to appear lovely in her sight, their
coaches, liveries, and themselves, all gay as on a monarch's birth-
day, to attract the eyes of this fair charmer, while she has the
pleasure to behold all languish for her that see her.

FREDERICK.

'Tis pretty to see with how much love the men regard her, and   310
how much envy the women.

WILLMORE.

What gallant has she?

BELVILE.

None, she's exposed to sale,[†] and four days in the week she's
yours — for so much a month.

WILLMORE.

The very thought of it quenches all manner of fire in me — yet 315
prithee let's see her.

BELVILE.

Let's first to dinner, and after that we'll pass the day as you
please — but at night ye must all be at my devotion.

WILLMORE.

I will not fail you.

302 Paduana] a woman from Padua

ACT II
Scene I. The Long Street

Enter Belvile and Frederick in masquing habits, and Willmore in his own
clothes, with a vizard in his hand.

WILLMORE.
But why thus disguised and muzzled?
BELVILE.
Because whatever extravagances we commit in these faces, our
own may not be obliged to answer 'em.
WILLMORE.
I should have changed my eternal buff too; but no matter, my lit-
tle gipsy would not have found me out then, for if she should
change hers, it is impossible I should know her, unless I should
hear her prattle. A pox on't, I cannot get her out of my head;
pray heaven, if ever I do see her again, she prove damnably ugly,
that I may fortify myself against her tongue.
BELVILE.
Have a care of love, for o'my conscience she was not of a quality
to give thee any hopes.
WILLMORE.
Pox on 'em, why do they draw a man in then? She has played
with my heart so, that 'twill never lie still till I have met with some
kind wench that will play the game out with me — oh, for my
arms full of soft, white, kind — woman — such as I fancy Angellica.
BELVILE.
This is her house, if you were but in stock to get admittance.
They have not dined yet; I perceive the picture is not out.

Enter Blunt.

WILLMORE.
I long to see the shadow of the fair substance; a man may gaze on
that for nothing.

Stage Direction: vizard] mask
4 buff] hard-wearing dull yellow leather used in soldiers' coats

BLUNT.

Colonel, thy hand — and thine, Fred. I have been an ass, a de-
luded fool, a very coxcomb from my birth till this hour, and
heartily repent my little faith.

BELVILE.

What the devil's the matter with thee, Ned?

BLUNT.[†]

Oh such a mistress[†] Fred, such a girl!   25

WILLMORE.

Ha! where?

FREDERICK.[†]

Ay, where!

BLUNT.[†]

So fond, so amorous, so toying and so fine! And all for sheer
love, ye rogue! Oh how she looked and kissed! And soothed my
heart from my bosom — I cannot think I was awake, and yet me-   30
thinks I see and feel her charms still — Fred, try if she have not
left the taste of her balmy kisses upon my lips.

Kisses him.

BELVILE.

Ha! Ha! Ha!

WILLMORE.[†]

Death, man, where is she?

BLUNT.[†]

What a dog was I to stay in dull England so long. How have I   35
laughed at the colonel when he sighed for love! But now the little
archer has revenged him! And by this one dart, I can guess at all
his joys, which then I took for fancies, mere dreams and fables.
Well, I'm resolved to sell all in Essex, and plant here for ever.

BELVILE.

What a blessing 'tis thou hast a mistress thou dar'st boast of, for I   40
know thy humour is rather to have a proclaimed clap than a secret amour.

---

36 little archer] Cupid
41 clap] venereal disease

WILLMORE.

> Dost know her name?

BLUNT.

> Her name? No, 'sheartlikins, what care I for names? She's fair!
> Young! Brisk and kind, even to ravishment! And what a pox care   45
> I for knowing her by any other title?

WILLMORE.

> Didst give her anything?

BLUNT.

> Give her! Ha, ha, ha! Why she's a person of quality — that's a
> good one, give her! 'Sheartlikins, dost think such creatures are to
> be bought? Or are we provided for such a purchase? Give her,   50
> quoth ye? Why, she presented me with this bracelet for the toy of
> a diamond I used to wear. No, gentlemen, Ned Blunt is not eve-
> rybody. She expects me again tonight.

WILLMORE.

> Egad, that's well; we'll all go.

BLUNT.

> Not a soul. No, gentlemen, you are wits; I am a dull country   55
> rogue, I.

FREDERICK.

> Well, sir, for all your person of quality, I shall be very glad to un-
> derstand your purse be secure; 'tis our whole estate at present,
> which we are loath to hazard in one bottom; come, sir, unlade.

BLUNT.

> Take the necessary trifle useless now to me, that am beloved by   60
> such a gentlewoman — 'sheartlikins, money! Here, take mine too.

FREDERICK.

> No, keep that to be cozened, that we may laugh.

WILLMORE.

> Cozened — death! Would I could meet with one that would cozen
> me of all the love I could spare tonight.

FREDERICK.

> Pox, 'tis some common whore, upon my life.   65

---

59 bottom] keel or hull of a ship; a cargo ship
62 cozened] cheated

BLUNT.

A whore! Yes, with such clothes! Such jewels! Such a house! Such furniture, and so attended! A whore!

BELVILE.

Why yes, sir, they are whores, though they'll neither entertain you with drinking, swearing, or bawdry; are whores in all those gay clothes and right jewels; are whores with those great houses 70 richly furnished with velvet beds, store of plate, handsome attendance and fine coaches; are whores, and errant ones.

WILLMORE.

Pox on't, where do these fine whores live?

BELVILE.

Where no rogues in office ycleped constables dare give 'em laws, nor the wine-inspired bullies of the town break their windows; 75 yet they are whores, though this Essex calf believe 'em persons of quality.

BLUNT.

'Sheartlikins, y'are all fools; there are things about this Essex calf that shall take with the ladies, beyond all your wit and parts — this shape and size, gentlemen, are not to be despised — my waist,[†] 80 too, tolerably long, with other inviting signs, that shall be nameless.

WILLMORE.

Egad, I believe he may have met with some person of quality that may be kind to him.

BELVILE.

Dost thou perceive any such tempting things about him, that 85 should make a fine woman, and of quality, pick him out from all mankind to throw away her youth and beauty upon, nay and her dear heart too! No, no, Angellica has raised the price too high.

WILLMORE.

May she languish for mankind till she die, and be damned for that one sin alone. 90

---

71 plate] silver-plated items
74 ycleped] called, named
76 Essex calf] fool; a native of Essex. Blunt's home county of Essex was famous for its calves.

Enter two bravoes, Biskey and Sebastian and up a great picture of Angellica's against the balcony, and two little ones at each side of the door.

BELVILE.

See there, the fair sign to the inn where a man may lodge that's fool enough to give her price.

Willmore gazes on the picture.

BLUNT.

'Sheartlikins, gentlemen, what's this!

BELVILE.

A famous courtesan, that's to be sold.

BLUNT.

How? To be sold! Nay then, I have nothing to say to her — sold! What impudence is practiced in this country? With what order and decency whoring's established here by virtue of the Inquisition. Come, let's begone, I'm sure we're no chapmen for this commodity.

FREDERICK.

Thou art none, I'm sure, unless thou could'st have her in thy bed at a price of a coach in the street.

WILLMORE.

How wondrous fair she is. A thousand crowns a month — by heaven, as many kingdoms were too little; a plague of this poverty — of which I ne'er complain but when it hinders my approach to beauty which virtue ne'er could purchase.

Turns from the picture.

BLUNT.

What's this? [*Reads.*]

A thousand crowns a month!

'Sheartlikins, here's a sum! Sure 'tis a mistake.

— Hark you friend, does she take or give so much by the month?

---

102 crown] gold coin, value 5 shillings

FREDERICK.

    A thousand crowns! Why 'tis a portion for the Infanta.   110

BLUNT.

    Harkee, friends, won't she trust?

BRAVO.

    This is a trade, sir, that cannot live by credit.

Enter Don Pedro in masquerade, followed by Stephano.

BELVILE.

    See, here's more company; let's walk off a while.

Exeunt English. Pedro reads.

Enter Angellica and Moretta in the balcony, and draw a silk curtain.

PEDRO.

    Fetch me a thousand crowns, I never wished to buy this beauty at
an easier rate.   115

Passes off.

ANGELLICA.

    Prithee what said those fellows to thee?

BRAVO.

    Madam, the first were admirers of beauty only, but no purchas-
ers; they were merry with your price and picture, laughed at the
sum, and so passed off.

ANGELLICA.

    No matter, I'm not displeased with their rallying; their wonder   120
feeds my vanity, and he that wishes but to buy gives me more
pride than he that gives my price can make my pleasure.

BRAVO.

    Madam, the last I knew through all his disguises to be Don Pe-
dro, nephew to the general, and who was with him in Pamplona.

---

110 Infanta] daughter of the Spanish king
111 harkee] hark ye, listen

ANGELLICA.

Don Pedro! My old gallant's nephew. When his uncle died he left
him a vast sum of money; it is he who was so in love with me at
Padua, and who used to make the general so jealous.

MORETTA.

Is this he that used to prance before our window, and take such
care to show himself an amorous ass? If I am not mistaken, he is
the likeliest man to give your price.

ANGELLICA.

The man is brave and generous, but of an humour so uneasy and
inconstant, that the victory over his heart is as soon lost as won, a
slave that can add little to the triumph of the conqueror. But inconstancy's the sin of all mankind; therefore I'm resolved that
nothing but gold shall charm my heart.

MORETTA.

I'm glad on't; 'tis only interest that women of our profession
ought to consider, though I wonder what has kept you from that
general disease of our sex so long, I mean that of being in love.

ANGELLICA.

A kind but sullen star under which I had the happiness to be
born. Yet I have had no time for love; the bravest and noblest of
mankind have purchased my favours at so dear a rate as if no
coin but gold were current with our trade — but here's Don Pedro again, fetch me my lute — for 'tis for him or Don Antonio the
viceroy's son, that I have spread my nets.

*Enter at one door Don Pedro, Stephano; Don Antonio and Diego (Page)‡ at
the other door, with people following him in masquerade, anticly attired,
some with music; they both go up to the picture.*

ANTONIO.

A thousand crowns! Had not the painter flattered her, I should
not think it dear.

PEDRO.

Flattered her! By heav'n, he cannot; I have seen the original, nor
is there one charm here more than adorns her face and eyes; all

---

125 gallant] fine gentleman; lover or paramour
146 dear] expensive
‡ stage direction added by editor

this soft and sweet, with a certain languishing air, that no artist can represent. 150

ANTONIO.

What I heard of her beauty before had fired my soul, but this confirmation of it has blown it to a flame.

PEDRO.

Ha!

PAGE.

Sir, I have known you throw away a thousand crowns on a worse face, and though y'are near your marriage, you may venture a lit- 155 tle love here. Florinda will not miss it.

PEDRO. [*Aside.*]

Ha! Florinda! Sure 'tis Antonio.

ANTONIO.

Florinda! Name not those distant joys; there's not one thought of her will check my passion here.

PEDRO.

Florinda scorned! And all my hopes defeated of the possession of Angellica. 160

A noise of a lute above. Antonio gazes up.

Her injuries, by heaven, he shall not boast of.

Song to a lute above.

SONG.

When Damon first began to love
He languished in a soft desire,
And knew not how the gods to move, 165
To lessen or increase his fire.
For Caelia in her charming eyes
Wore all love's sweets, and all his cruelties.
II.
But as beneath a shade he lay,
Weaving of flow'rs for Caelia's hair, 170
She chanced to lead her flock that way,
And saw the am'rous shepherd there.
She gazed around upon the place,
And saw the grove (resembling night)
To all the joys of love invite, 175

Whilst guilty smiles and blushes dressed her face.
At this the bashful youth all transport grew,
And with kind force he taught the virgin how
To yield what all his sighs could never do.

*Angellica throws open the curtains and bows to Antonio, who pulls off his
vizard and bows and blows up kisses.*

Pedro unseen looks in's face.

ANTONIO.
By Heav'n she's charming fair!   18

PEDRO.
'Tis he; the false Antonio!

ANTONIO.   [*To the bravo.*]
Friend, where must I pay my offering of love?
My thousand crowns I mean.

PEDRO.
That offering I have designed to make.
And yours will come too late.   18

ANTONIO.
Prithee begone, I shall grow angry else.
And then thou art not safe.

PEDRO.
My anger may be fatal, sir, as yours,
And he that enters here may prove this truth.

ANTONIO.
I know not who thou art, but I am sure thou'rt worth my killing,   19
for aiming at Angellica.

They draw and fight. Enter Willmore and Blunt who draw and part 'em.

BLUNT.
'Sheartlikins, here's fine doings.

WILLMORE.
Tilting for the wench, I'm sure — nay, gad, if that would win her,
I have as good a sword as the best of ye. Put up — put up, and
take another time and place, for this is designed for lovers only.   19

They all put up.

PEDRO.

    We are prevented; dare you meet me tomorrow on the Molo?

    For I've a title to a better quarrel,

    That of Florinda, in whose credulous heart

    Thou'st made an int'rest and destroyed my hopes.

ANTONIO.

    Dare!   200

    I'll meet thee there as early as the day.

PEDRO.

    We will come thus disguised that whosoever chance to get the
better, he may escape unknown.

ANTONIO.

    It shall be so.

Exeunt Pedro and Stephano.

    Who should this rival be? Unless the English colonel, of whom   205
I've often heard Don Pedro speak; it must be he, and time he
were removed, who lays claim to all my happiness.

Willmore having gazed all this while on the picture, pulls down a little one.

WILLMORE.

    This posture's loose and negligent,

    The sight on't would beget a warm desire

    In souls whom impotence and age had chilled.   210

    This must along with me.

BRAVO.

    What means this rudeness, sir? Restore the picture.

ANTONIO.

    Ha! Rudeness committed to the fair Angellica! Restore the pic-
ture, sir —

WILLMORE.

    Indeed I will not, sir.   215

ANTONIO.

    By heaven, but you shall.

---

193 tilting for] fighting for; charging on horseback against an opponent with a lance
196 the Molo] pier; from "môle" (Fr.).

WILLMORE.

> Nay, do not show your sword; if you do, by this dear beauty — I will show mine too.

ANTONIO.

> What right can you pretend to't?

WILLMORE.

> That of possession, which I will maintain — you perhaps have a thousand[†] crowns to give for the original.

ANTONIO.

> No matter, sir, you shall restore the picture.

Angellica and Moretta above.

ANGELLICA.

> Oh Moretta! What's the matter?

ANTONIO.

> Or leave your life behind.

WILLMORE.

> Death! you lie — I will do neither.

They fight; the Spaniards join with Antonio; Blunt laying on like mad.

ANGELLICA.

> Hold, I command you, if for me you fight.[†]

They leave off and bow.

WILLMORE.

> How heavenly fair she is! Ah, plague of her price.

ANGELLICA.

> You sir, in buff, you that appear a soldier, that first began this insolence —

WILLMORE.

> 'Tis true, I did so, if you call it insolence for a man to preserve himself. I saw your charming picture and was wounded; quite through my soul each pointed beauty ran, and, wanting a thousand crowns to procure my remedy, I laid this little picture to my bosom — which if you cannot allow me, I'll resign.

ANGELLICA.

> No, you may keep the trifle.

ANTONIO.

> You shall first ask me leave, and this.

Fight again as before.

Enter Belvile and Frederick who join with the English.

ANGELLICA.

Hold! Will you ruin me? Biskey — Sebastian — part 'em.

The Spaniards are beaten off.

MORETTA.

Oh madam, we're undone. A pox upon that rude fellow, he's set on to ruin us; we shall never see good days till all these fighting poor rogues are sent to the galleys.   240

Enter Belvile, Blunt, Frederick, and Willmore with's shirt bloody.

BLUNT.

'Sheartlikins, beat me at this sport, and I'll ne'er wear sword more.

BELVILE.

The devil's in thee for a mad fellow; thou art always one at an unlucky adventure — come, let's begone whilst we're safe, and remember these are Spaniards, a sort of people that know how to   245
revenge an affront.

FREDERICK.   [*To Willmore.*]

You bleed! I hope you are not wounded.

WILLMORE.

Not much — a plague on your dons; if they fight no better they'll ne'er recover Flanders. What the devil was't to them that I took down the picture?   250

BLUNT.

Took it! 'Sheartlikins, we'll have the great one too; 'tis ours by conquest. Prithee help me up and I'll pull it down —

ANGELLICA.

Stay sir, and ere you affront me farther, let me know how you durst commit this outrage — to you I speak, sir, for you appear a gentleman.   255

WILLMORE.

To me, madam — gentlemen, your servant.

Belvile stays him.

BELVILE.

Is the devil in thee? Dost know the danger of entering the house of an incensed courtesan?

WILLMORE.

    I thank you for your care — but there are other matters in hand, there are, though we have no great temptation. Death! Let me go.

FREDERICK.

    Yes, to your lodging if you will, but not in here. Damn these gay harlots — by this hand I'll have as sound and handsome a whore for a patacoon — death, man, she'll murder thee.

WILLMORE.

    Oh! Fear me not, shall I not venture where a beauty calls? A lovely charming beauty! For fear of danger! When by Heaven there's none so great as to long for her whilst I want money[†] to purchase her.

FREDERICK.[†]

    Therefore 'tis loss of time unless you had the thousand crowns to pay.

WILLMORE.

    It may be she may give a favour; at least I shall have the pleasure of saluting her when I enter, and when I depart.

BELVILE.

    Pox, she'll as soon lie with thee as kiss thee, and sooner stab than do either — you shall not go.

ANGELLICA.

    Fear not sir, all I have to wound with is my eyes.

BLUNT.

    Let him go. 'Sheartlikins, I believe the gentlewoman means well.

BELVILE.

    Well, take thy fortune; we'll expect you in the next street — farewell, fool — farewell —

WILLMORE.

    Bye[†] colonel —

                Goes in.

FREDERICK.

    The rogue's stark mad for a wench.

                Exeunt.

---

264 patacoon] Spanish coin; value in seventeenth century, 4s.8d.

Scene II. A fine Chamber.

Enter Willmore, Angellica and Moretta.

ANGELLICA.

Insolent sir, how durst you pull down my picture?

WILLMORE.

Rather, how durst you set it up, to tempt poor amorous mortals
with so much excellence, which I find you have but too well consulted by the unmerciful price you set upon't. Is all this heaven of
beauty shown to move despair in those that cannot buy? And can   5
you think th'effects of that despair should be less extravagant
than I have shown?

ANGELLICA.

I sent for you to ask my pardon sir, not to aggravate your crime
— I thought I should have seen you at my feet imploring it.

WILLMORE.

You are deceived; I came to rail at you, and rail such truths too,   10
as shall let you see the vanity of that pride which taught you how ·
to set such price on sin. For such it is, whilst that which is love's
due is meanly bartered for.

ANGELLICA.

Ha! ha! ha! Alas, good captain, what pity 'tis your edifying doctrine will do no good upon me — Moretta! Fetch the gentleman a   15
glass, and let him survey himself, to see what charms he has —
[*Aside in a soft tone*] and guess my business.

MORETTA.

He knows himself of old; I believe those breeches and he have
been acquainted ever since he was beaten at Worcester.

ANGELLICA.

Nay, do not abuse the poor creature —   20

---

19 Worcester] The Battle of Worcester (1651) was the final defeat of Prince Charles by
the Parliamentary forces, after which he fled to the continent.

MORETTA.

Good weather-beaten corporal, will you march off? We have no
need of your doctrine, though you have of our charity, but at
present we have no scraps, we can afford no kindness for God's
sake; in fine, sirrah, the price is too high i'th'mouth for you,
therefore troop, I say.

WILLMORE.

Here, good forewoman of the shop, serve me, and I'll be gone.

MORETTA.

Keep it to pay your laundress, your linen stinks of the gunroom;
for here's no selling by retail.

WILLMORE.

Thou hast sold plenty of thy stale ware at a cheap rate.

MORETTA.

Ay, the more silly kind heart I, but this is an age wherein beauty
is at higher rates. In fine, you know the price of this.

WILLMORE.

I grant you 'tis here — set down a thousand crowns a month —
pray, how much may come to my share for a pistole? Bawd, take
your black lead and sum it up, that I may have a pistole's[†]worth
of this vain gay thing,[†] and I'll trouble you no more.

MORETTA.

Pox on him, he'll fret me to death — abominable fellow, I tell
thee, we only sell by the whole piece.

WILLMORE.

'Tis very hard, the whole cargo or nothing. Faith, madam, my
stock will not reach it; I cannot be your chapman — yet I have
countrymen in town, merchants of love like me; I'll see if they'll
put in for a share. We cannot lose much by it, and what we have
no use for, we'll sell upon the Friday's mart at "Who gives more?"
I am studying, madam, how to purchase you, though at present I
am unprovided of money.

ANGELLICA. [Aside][‡]

Sure, this from any other man would anger me — nor shall he
know the conquest he has made

---

24 high i'th'mouth] above one's rank; elevated
33 pistole]gold coin; value between 16s.6d. and 18s .
34 black lead] pencil

— Poor angry man, how I despise this railing.
WILLMORE.

Yes, I am poor — but I am a gentleman,
And one that scorns this baseness which you practice;
Poor as I am, I would not sell myself,   50
No, not to gain your charming high prized person.
Though I admire you strangely for your beauty,
Yet I contemn your mind.
And yet I would at any rate enjoy you
At your own rate — but cannot. See here   55
The only sum I can command on earth;
I know not where to eat when this is gone.
Yet such a slave I am to love and beauty
This last reserve I'll sacrifice to enjoy you.
Nay, do not frown, I know you're to be bought,   60
And would be bought by me, by me,
For a mean trifling sum if I could pay it down;
Which happy knowledge I will still repeat,
And lay it to my heart; it has a virtue in't,
And soon will cure those wounds your eyes have made. 65
And yet — there's something so divinely powerful there —
Nay, I will gaze — to let you see my strength.

Holds her, looks on her, and pauses and sighs.

By heav'n, bright creature — I would not for the world
Thy fame were half so fair as is thy face.

Turns her away from him.

ANGELLICA. [*Aside.*]

His words go through me to the very soul.   70
— If you have nothing else to say to me —
WILLMORE.

Yes, you shall hear how infamous you are —
For which I do not hate thee —
But that secures my heart, and all the flames it feels

---

53 contemn] have contempt for

Are but so many lusts —
I know it by their sudden bold intrusion.
The fire's impatient and betrays, 'tis false —
For had it been the purer flame of love,
I should have pined and languished at your feet,
Ere found the impudence to have discovered it.
I now dare stand your scorn, and your denial.

MORETTA.

Sure she's bewitched,† that she can stand thus tamely and hear his saucy railing — sirrah, will you be gone?

ANGELLICA.   [*To Moretta.*]

How dare you take this liberty? Withdraw.
—Pray tell me, sir, are not you guilty of the same mercenary crime? When a lady is proposed to you for a wife, you never ask how fair, discreet, or virtuous she is, but what's her fortune — which if but small, you cry, "She will not do my business" and basely leave her, though† she languish for you — say, is not this as poor?

WILLMORE.

It is a barbarous custom, which I will scorn to defend in our sex, and do despise in yours.

ANGELLICA.

Thou'rt a brave fellow! Put up thy gold, and know,
That were thy fortune as large as thy soul,
Thou should'st not buy my love,
Couldst thou forget those mean effects of vanity
Which set me out to sale, and, as a lover, prize my yielding joys.
Canst thou believe they'll be entirely thine,
Without considering they were mercenary?

WILLMORE.

I cannot tell, I must bethink me first. [*Aside.*] — Ha — death, I'm going to believe her.

ANGELLICA.

Prithee confirm that faith — or if thou canst not — flatter me a little, 'twill please me from thy mouth.

WILLMORE.   [*Aside.*]

Curse on thy charming tongue! Dost thou return
My feigned contempt with so much subtlety?

---

92 put up] put away

— Thou'st found the easiest way into my heart,   105
Though I yet know that all thou say'st is false.

Turning from her in rage.

ANGELLICA.
By all that's good, 'tis real;
I never loved before, though oft a mistress.
Shall my first vows be slighted?
WILLMORE.   [*Aside.*]
What can she mean?   110
ANGELLICA.   [*In an angry tone.*]
I find you cannot credit me.
WILLMORE.
I know you take me for an errant ass,
An ass that may be soothed into belief
And then be used at pleasure;
But madam, I have been so often cheated   115
By perjured soft deluding hypocrites,
That I've no faith left for the cozening sex;
Especially for women of your trade.
ANGELLICA.
The low esteem you have of me, perhaps
May bring my heart again: 120
For I have pride, that yet surmounts my love.

She turns with pride; he holds her.

WILLMORE.
Throw off this pride, this enemy to bliss,
And show the pow'r of love; 'tis with those arms
I can be only vanquished, made a slave.
ANGELLICA.
Is all my mighty expectation vanished?   125
No, I will not hear thee talk — thou hast a charm
In every word that draws my heart away.
And all the thousand trophies I designed
Thou hast undone — why art thou soft?
Thy looks are bravely rough, and meant for war.   130
Could'st thou not storm on still?
I then perhaps had been as free as thou.

WILLMORE.   [*Aside.*]

    Death, how she throws her fire about my soul!
    — Take heed, fair creature, how you raise my hopes,
    Which once assumed pretends to all dominion.   13
    There's not a joy thou hast in store,
    I shall not then command.
    For which I'll pay thee back my soul, my life!
    Come, let's begin th'account this happy minute!

ANGELLICA.

    And will you pay me then the price I ask?   14

WILLMORE.

    Oh, why dost thou draw me from an awful worship,
    By showing thou art no divinity?
    Conceal the fiend, and show me the angel!
    Keep me but ignorant, and I'll be devout
    And pay my vows for ever at this shrine.   14

Kneels and kisses her hand.

ANGELLICA.

    The pay I mean, is but thy love for mine.
    Can you give that?

WILLMORE.

    Entirely — come, let's withdraw! Where I'll renew my vows — and
    breathe 'em with such ardour thou shalt not doubt my zeal.

ANGELLICA.

    Thou hast a pow'r too strong to be resisted.   15

Exeunt Willmore and Angellica.

MORETTA.

    Now my curse go with you — is all our project fallen to this? To
    love the only enemy to our trade? Nay, to love such a shameroon,
    a very beggar, nay a pirate beggar, whose business is to rifle, and

---

be gone, a no-purchase, no-pay tatterdemalion and English
picaroon. A rogue that fights for daily drink, and takes a pride in   155
being loyally lousy — oh, I could curse now, if I durst. This is the
fate of most whores.

Trophies, which from believing fops we win,
Are spoils to those who cozen us again.

---

154 tatterdemalion] a person with tattered clothes
155 picaroon] rogue, pirate
156 lousy] to have lice

ACT III.

Scene I. A Street.

*Enter Florinda, Valeria, Hellena, in antic different dresses from what they
were in before. Callis attending.*

FLORINDA.

I wonder what should make my brother in so ill a humour? I
hope he has not found out our ramble this morning.

HELLENA.

No, if he had, we should have heard on't at both ears, and have
been mewed up this afternoon; which I would not for the world
should have happened — hey ho, I'm as sad as a lover's lute.   5

VALERIA.

Well, methinks we have learnt this trade of gypsies as readily as if
we have been bred upon the road to Loreto;† and yet I did so
fumble when I told the stranger his fortune, that I was afraid I
should have told my own and yours by mistake — but methinks
Hellena has been very serious ever since.   1

FLORINDA.

I would give my garters she were in love, to be revenged upon
her for abusing me — how is't, Hellena?

HELLENA.

Ah — would I had never seen my mad monsieur — and yet for all
your laughing, I am not in love — and yet this small acquaintance,
o' my conscience, will never out of my head.   1

VALERIA.

Ha, ha, ha — I laugh to think how thou art fitted with a lover, a
fellow that I warrant loves every new face he sees.

HELLENA.

Hum — he has not kept his word with me here — and may be
taken up — that thought is not very pleasant to me — what the
deuce should this be now, that I feel?   2

VALERIA.

What is't like?

---

4 mewed] caged; from "mew," a cage for hawks
7 Loreto] a city in Italy famous as a place of pilgrimage

HELLENA.

Nay, the lord knows — but if I should be hanged, I cannot choose but be angry and afraid when I think that mad fellow should be in love with any body but me — what to think of myself, I know not — would I could meet with some true damned gypsy, that I might know my fortune.   25

VALERIA.

Know it! Why there's nothing so easy; thou wilt love this wandering inconstant till thou find'st thyself hanged about his neck, and then be as mad to get free again.

FLORINDA.

Yes, Valeria, we shall see her bestride his baggage horse, and fol-   30
low him to the campaign.

HELLENA.

So, so, now you are provided for there's no care taken of poor me — but since you have set my heart a-wishing — I am resolved to know for what; I will not die of the pip, so I will not.

FLORINDA.

Art thou mad to talk so? Who will like thee well enough to have   35
thee, that hears what a mad wench thou art?

HELLENA.

Like me! I don't intend every he that likes me shall have me, but he that I like; I should have stayed in the nunnery still, if I had liked my lady Abbess as well as she liked me — no, I came thence not (as my wise brother imagines) to take an eternal farewell of the world, but to love and to be beloved, and I will be beloved, or   40
I'll get one of your men, so I will.

VALERIA.

Am I put into the number of lovers?

HELLENA.

You? Why coz, I know thou'rt too good-natured to leave us in any design; thou would[†] venture a cast, though thou comest off a   45
loser, especially with such a gamester. I observe your man, and your willing ear incline that way; and if you are not a lover, 'tis an art soon learnt — that I find.

Sighs.

---

34 the pip] depression, ill temper

FLORINDA.

I wonder how you learnt to love so easily; I had a thousand[†]
charms to meet my eyes and ears ere I could yield, and 'twas the   50
knowledge of Belvile's merit, not the surprising person, took my
soul — thou art too rash, to give a heart at first sight.

HELLENA.

Hang your considering lover; I never thought beyond the fancy
that 'twas a very pretty, idle, silly kind of pleasure to pass one's
time with, to write little soft nonsensical billets, and with great   55
difficulty and danger receive answers in which I shall have my
beauty praised, my wit admired, (though little or none) and have
the vanity and power to know I am desirable; then I have the
more inclination that way, because I am to be a nun, and so shall
not be suspected to have any such earthly thoughts about me —   60
but when I walk thus — and sigh thus — they'll think my mind's
upon my monastery, and cry how happy 'tis she's so resolved.
But not a word[†] of man.

FLORINDA.

What a mad creature's this?

HELLENA.

I'll warrant, if my brother hears either of you sigh, he cries   65
(gravely) — I fear you have the indiscretion to be in love, but take
heed of the honour of our house, and your own unspotted fame,
and so he conjures on till he has laid the soft-winged god in your
hearts, or broke the bird's nest — but see, here comes your lover,
but where's my inconstant? Let's step aside, and we may learn   70
something.

Go aside.

Enter Belvile, Frederick and Blunt.

BELVILE.

What means this! The picture's taken in.

BLUNT.

It may be the wench is good-natured, and will be kind gratis.
Your friend's a proper handsome fellow.

---

55 billets] love notes

BELVILE.

    I rather think she has cut his throat and is fled: I am mad he   75
should throw himself into dangers — pox on't, I shall want him
too at night — let's knock and ask for him.

HELLENA.

    My heart goes a-pit a-pat, for fear 'tis my man they talk of.†

Knock; Moretta above.

MORETTA.

    What would you have!

BELVILE.

    Tell the stranger that entered here about two hours ago that his   80
friends stay here for him.

MORETTA.

    A curse upon him for Moretta; would he were at the devil — but
he's coming to you.

Enter Willmore.†

HELLENA.

    Ay, ay,† 'tis he! Oh how this vexes me.

BELVILE.

    And how and how dear lad, has fortune smiled? Are we to break   85
her windows? Or raise up altars to her, hah?

WILLMORE.

    Does not my fortune sit triumphant on my brow? Dost not see
the little wanton god there all gay and smiling? Have I not an air
about my face and eyes that distinguish me from the crowd of
common lovers? By heaven, Cupid's quiver has not half so many   90
darts as her eyes! Oh, such a bona roba! To sleep in her arms is
lying in fresco, all perfumed air about me.

HELLENA.   [*Aside.*]

    Here's fine encouragement for me to fool on.

---

91 bona roba] literally, good dress; figuratively, compliant woman, courtesan
92 in fresco] in fresh air, outside

WILLMORE.

> Harkee, where didst thou purchase that rich Canary we drank to- | 95
> day! Tell me, that I may adore the spigot and sacrifice to the
> butt! The juice was divine into which I must dip my rosary, and
> then bless all things that I would have bold or fortunate.

BELVILE.

> Well sir, let's go take a bottle, and hear the story of your success.

FREDERICK.

> Would not French wine do better?

WILLMORE.

> Damn the hungry balderdash, cheerful sack has a generous vir- | 100
> tue in't inspiring a successful confidence; gives eloquence to the
> tongue, and vigour to the soul, and has in a few hours completed
> all my hopes and wishes! There's nothing left to raise a new de-
> sire in me — come let's be gay and wanton — and gentlemen,
> study, study what you want, for here are friends that will supply | 105
> gentlemen — hark! What a charming sound they make — 'tis he
> and she gold† whilst here, and shall beget new pleasures every
> moment.

BLUNT.

> But harkee sir, you are not married, are you?

WILLMORE.

> All the honey of matrimony, but none of the sting, friend. | 110

BLUNT.

> 'Sheartlikins, thou'rt a fortunate rogue!

WILLMORE.

> I am so sir, let these — inform you! Ha, how sweetly they chime!
> Pox of poverty, it makes a man a slave, makes wit and honour
> sneak, my soul grew lean and rusty for want of credit.

BLUNT.

> 'Sheartlikins, this I like well, it looks like my lucky bargain! Oh | 115
> how I long for the approach of my squire, that is to conduct me
> to her house again. Why — here's two provided for.

---

94 Canary] wine from the Canary Islands; first of a series of metaphors drawn from
  winemaking and drinking
96 butt] cask for wine or ale
100 balderdash] a mixture of alcoholic drinks
100 sack] white wine from Spain and Canary Islands

FREDERICK.

By this light y'are happy men.

BLUNT.

Fortune is pleased to smile on us, gentlemen — to smile on us.

Enter Sancho and pulls down Blunt by the sleeve.

SANCHO.

Sir, my lady expects you —   120

They go aside.

She has remov'd all that might oppose your will and pleasure — and is impatient till you come.

BLUNT.

Sir, I'll attend you — oh, the happiest rogue! I'll take no leave, lest† they either dog me, or stay me.

Exit with Sancho.

BELVILE.

But then the little gypsy is forgot?   125

WILLMORE.

A mischief on thee for putting her into my thoughts. I had quite forgot her else, and this night's debauch had drunk her quite down.

HELLENA.

Had it so, good captain!

Claps him on the back.

WILLMORE. [*Aside.*]

Hah! I hope she did not hear me.   130

HELLENA.

What, afraid of such a champion?

WILLMORE.

Oh! you're a fine lady of your word, are you not? To make a man languish a whole day —

HELLENA.

In tedious search of me.

WILLMORE.

Egad child, thou'rt in the right; had'st thou seen what a melancholy dog I have been ever since I was a lover, how I have walked
the streets like a Capuchin with my hands in my sleeves — faith,
sweetheart, thou would'st pity me.

HELLENA.   [*Aside*]†

Now if I should be hanged I can't be angry with him, he dissem-
bles so heartily
— alas, good captain, what pains you have taken — now were I ungrateful not to reward so true a servant.

WILLMORE.

Poor soul! That's kindly said; I see thou barest† a conscience —
come then, for a beginning show me thy dear face.

HELLENA.

I'm afraid, my small acquaintance, you have been staying that
swinging stomach you boasted this morning; I then remember
my little collation would have gone down with you, without the
sauce of a handsome face — is your stomach so queasy now?

WILLMORE.

Faith, long fasting, child, spoils a man's appetite — yet if you
durst treat, I could so lay about me still —

HELLENA.

And would you fall to, before a priest says grace?

WILLMORE.

Oh fie, fie, what an old, out of fashioned thing hast thou named?
Thou could'st not dash me more out of countenance should'st
thou show me an ugly face.

*Whilst he is seemingly courting Hellena, enter Angellica, Moretta, Biskey
and Sebastian, all in masquerade; Angellica sees Willmore and stares.*

ANGELLICA.

Heavens 'tis† he! And passionately fond to see another woman.

MORETTA.

What could you less expect from such a swaggerer?

ANGELLICA.

Expect! As much as I paid him, a heart entire

---

137 Capuchin] a friar of the order of St. Francis
147 collation] light meal

Which I had pride enough to think when ere I gave,
It would have raised the man above the vulgar,
Made him all soul, and that all soft and constant.   160

HELLENA.

You see, captain, how willing I am to be friends with you, till time
and ill luck make us lovers, and ask you the question first, rather
than put your modesty to the blush by asking me (for alas!) I
know you captains are such strict men, and such severe observers
of your vows to chastity, that 'twill be hard to prevail with your   165
tender conscience to marry a young willing maid.

WILLMORE.

Do not abuse me, for fear I should take thee at thy word, and
marry thee indeed, which I'm sure will be revenge sufficient.

HELLENA.

O' my conscience, that will be our destiny, because we are both
of one humour; I am as inconstant as you, for I have considered,   170
captain, that a handsome woman has a great deal to do whilst her
face is good, for then is our harvest-time to gather friends; and
should I in these days of my youth catch a fit of foolish constancy, I were undone; 'tis loitering by daylight in our great jour-
ney. Therefore, I declare I'll allow but one year for love, one year   175
for indifference, and one year for hate — and then — go hang
yourself — for I profess myself the gay, the kind, and the inconstant — the devil's in't if this won't please you.

WILLMORE.

Oh most damnably — I have a heart with a hole quite through it
too; no prison mine to keep a mistress in.   180

ANGELLICA.   [*Aside.*]

Perjured man! How I believe thee now.

HELLENA.

Well, I see our business as well as humours are alike; yours to
cozen as many maids as will trust you, and I as many men as have
faith — see if I have not as desperate a lying look as you can have
for the heart of you.   185

Pulls off her vizard: he starts.

— How do you like it, captain?

WILLMORE.

Like it! By heaven, I never saw so much beauty! Oh the charms of
those sprightly black eyes! That strangely fair face, full of smiles

and dimples! Those soft round melting cherry lips! And small even white teeth! Not to be expressed, but silently adored! Oh, one look more! And strike me dumb, or I shall repeat nothing else till I'm mad.   190

He seems to court her to pull off her vizard: she refuses.

ANGELLICA.
I can endure no more — nor is it fit to interrupt him, for if I do, my jealousy has so destroyed my reason, I shall undo him — therefore I'll retire — [*To one of her bravoes.*] and you, Sebastian,   195
follow that woman, and learn who 'tis; [*To the other bravo.*] while you tell the fugitive, I would speak to him instantly.

Exit.

This while Florinda is talking to Belvile, who stands sullenly. Frederick courting Valeria.

VALERIA.
Prithee, dear stranger, be not so sullen, for though you have lost your love, you see my friend frankly offers you hers to play with in the meantime.   200
BELVILE.
Faith, madam, I am sorry I can't play at her game.
FREDERICK.
Pray leave your intercession, and mind your own affair. They'll better agree apart; he's a modest sigher in company, but alone no woman scapes him.
FLORINDA.
Sure he does but rally — yet if it should be true — I'll tempt him   205
farther. Believe me, noble stranger, I'm no common mistress, and for a little proof on't, wear this jewel — nay, take it, sir, 'tis right, and bills of exchange may sometimes miscarry.
BELVILE.
Madam, why am I chose out of all mankind to be the object of your bounty?   210

---

208 bills of exchange] written promises of future payment

VALERIA.

There's another civil question asked.

FREDERICK.

Pox of's modesty, it spoils his own markets and hinders mine.

FLORINDA.

Sir, from my window, I have often seen you, and women of my
quality have so few opportunities for love, that we ought to lose[†]
none.   215

FREDERICK.

Ay, this is something! Here's a woman! When shall I be blessed
with so much kindness from your fair mouth?

[*Aside to Belvile*] — Take the jewel, fool.

BELVILE.

You tempt me strangely, madam, every way —

FLORINDA.   [*Aside.*]

So, if I find him false, my whole repose is gone.   220

BELVILE.

And but for a vow I've made to a very fair[†] lady, this goodness
has subdued me.

FREDERICK.

Pox on't, be kind, in pity to me be kind, for I am to thrive here
but as you treat her friend.

HELLENA.

Tell me what you did in yonder house, and I'll unmask.   225

WILLMORE.

Yonder house — oh — I went to — a — to — why, there's a friend
of mine lives there.

HELLENA.

What, a she, or a he friend?

WILLMORE.

A man, upon honour! A man — a she friend — no, no, madam,
you have done my business I thank you.   230

HELLENA.

And was't your man friend that had more darts in's eyes than Cupid carries in's whole budget of arrows?

WILLMORE.

So —

---

232 budget] wallet, leather bag

HELLENA.

Ah, such a bona roba! To be in her arms is lying in fresco, all perfumed air about me — was this your man friend too?

WILLMORE.

So —

HELLENA.

That gave you the he and the she gold, that begets young pleasures?

WILLMORE.

Well, well, madam, then you see there are ladies in the world that will not be cruel — there are, madam, there are —

HELLENA.

And there be men too, as fine, wild, inconstant fellows as yourself, there be, captain, there be, if you go to that now — therefore I'm resolved —

WILLMORE.

Oh!

HELLENA.

To see your face no more —

WILLMORE.

Oh!

HELLENA.

Till tomorrow.

WILLMORE.

Egad, you frighted me.

HELLENA.

Nor then neither, unless you'll swear never to see that lady more.

WILLMORE.

See her! — Why, never to think of womankind again.

HELLENA.

Kneel — and swear —

Kneels, she gives him her hand.

WILLMORE.

I do, never to think — to see — to love — nor lie — with any but thy self.

HELLENA.

Kiss the book.

WILLMORE.

Oh, most religiously.

Kisses her hand.

HELLENA.

Now what a wicked creature am I, to damn a proper fellow.

CALLIS.   [*To Florinda.*]

Madam, I'll stay no longer, 'tis e'en dark.

FLORINDA.

However sir, I'll leave this with you — that when I'm gone, you may repent the opportunity you have lost by your modesty.

Gives him the jewel which is her picture, and exits. He gazes after her.

WILLMORE.

'Twill be an age till tomorrow — and till then I will most impatiently expect you. Adieu, my dear pretty angel.   260

Exeunt all the women.

BELVILE.

Ha! Florinda's picture — 'twas she herself — what a dull dog was I! I would have given the world for one minute's discourse with her.

FREDERICK.

This comes of your modesty! Ah, pox o' your vow, 'twas ten to one, but we had lost the jewel by't.   265

BELVILE.

Willmore! The blessed'st opportunity lost! Florinda! Friends! Florinda!

WILLMORE.

Ah rogue! Such black eyes! Such a face! Such a mouth! Such teeth! And so much wit!

BELVILE.

All, all, and a thousand charms besides.   270

WILLMORE.

Why, dost thou know her?

BELVILE.

Know her! Ay, ay, and a pox take me with all my heart for being modest.

WILLMORE.

But harkee, friend of mine, are you my rival? And have I been only beating the bush all this while?   275

BELVILE.

I understand thee not — I'm mad — see here —

Shows the picture.

WILLMORE.

Ha! Whose picture's this? 'Tis a fine wench!

FREDERICK.

The colonel's mistress,[†] sir.

WILLMORE.

Oh, oh, here — I thought't had been another prize — come, come, a bottle will set thee right again.

Gives the picture back.

BELVILE.

I am content to try, and by that time 'twill be late enough for our design.

WILLMORE.

Agreed.

Love does all day the soul's great empire keep
But wine at night lulls the soft god asleep.

Exeunt.

Scene II.
Lucetta's House.

Enter Blunt and Lucetta with a light.

LUCETTA.

Now we are safe and free; no fears of the coming home of my old jealous husband, which made me a little thoughtful when you came in first — but now love is all the business of my soul.

BLUNT. [*Aside.*]

I am transported! Pox on't, that I had but some fine things to say to her, such as lovers use — I was a fool not to learn of Frederick a little by heart before I came — something I must say —

— 'Sheartlikins, sweet soul! I am not used to compliment, but I'm an honest gentleman, and thy humble servant.

LUCETTA.

    I have nothing to pay for so great a favour, but such a love as
cannot but be great, since at first sight of that sweet face and   10
shape, it made me your absolute captive.

BLUNT.

    Kind heart! How prettily she talks! [*Aside.*] Egad, I'll show her
husband a Spanish trick; send him out of the world and marry
her. She's damnably in love with me, and will ne'er mind settle-
ments, and so there's that saved.   15

LUCETTA.

    Well sir, I'll go and undress me, and be with you instantly.

BLUNT.

    Make haste then, for 'sheartlikins, dear soul, thou canst not guess
at the pain of a longing lover, when his joys are drawn within the
compass of a few minutes.

LUCETTA.

    You speak my sense, and I'll make haste to prove it.   20

Exit.

BLUNT.

    'Tis a rare girl! And this one night's enjoyment with her will be
worth all the days I ever passed in Essex. Would she would go
with me into England; though to say truth, there's plenty of
whores already. But a pox on 'em, they are such mercenary —
prodigal whores, that they want such a one as this that's free and   25
generous to give 'em good examples. Why, what a house she has,
how rich and fine!

Enter Sancho[‡]

SANCHO.

    Sir, my lady has sent me to conduct you to her chamber.

---

14 settlements] financial arrangements which are part of a marriage contract

BLUNT.

Sir, I shall be proud to follow — here's one of her servants too! 'Sheartlikins, by this garb and gravity, he might be a justice of 30 peace in Essex, and is but a pimp here.

Exeunt.

Scene III   III

The scene changes to a chamber with an alcove bed in't, a table, etc. Lucetta in bed. Enter Sancho and Blunt, who takes the candle of Sancho at the door.

SANCHO.

Sir, my commission reaches no farther.

BLUNT.

Sir, I'll excuse your compliment — what, in bed my sweet mistress?

LUCETTA.

You see, I still outdo you in kindness.

BLUNT.

And thou shalt see what haste I'll make to quit scores — oh, the 5 luckiest rogue!

He undresses himself.

LUCETTA.

Should you be false or cruel now!

BLUNT.

False! 'Sheartlikins, what dost thou take me for? A Jew? An insensible heathen? A pox of thy old jealous husband; an he were dead, egad, sweet soul, it should be none of my fault if I did not 10 marry thee.

LUCETTA.

It never should be mine.

BLUNT.

Good soul! I'm the fortunatest dog!

---

9 an] if

LUCETTA.

Are you not undressed yet?

BLUNT.

As much as my impatience will permit.   15

Goes toward the bed in his shirt, drawers, etc.†

LUCETTA.

Hold, sir, put out the light, it may betray us else.

BLUNT.

Anything, I need no other light but that of thine eyes! 'Sheartlikins, there I think I had it.

Puts out the candle, the bed descends, he gropes about to find it.

— Why — why — where am I got? What, not yet? Where are you
sweetest? Ah, the rogue's silent now — a pretty love-trick this —   20
how she'll laugh at me anon! You need not, my dear rogue! You
need not! I'm all on fire already — come, come, now call me in
pity. Sure I'm enchanted! I have been round the chamber, and
can find neither woman, nor bed — I locked the door, I'm sure
she cannot go that way — or if she could, the bed could not.   25
Enough, enough, my pretty wanton, do not carry the jest too far —
[*Lights on a trap, and is let down.*] Ha, betrayed! Dogs! Rogues!
Pimps! Help! Help!

Enter Lucetta, Phillippo, and Sancho with a light.

PHILLIPPO. ,

Ha, ha, ha, he's dispatched† finely.

LUCETTA.

Now, sir, had I been coy, we had missed of this booty.   30

PHILLIPPO.

Nay, when I saw't was a substantial fool, I was mollified; but
when you dote upon a serenading coxcomb, upon a face, fine
clothes, and a lute, it makes me rage.

Stage Direction: bed descends] presumably through a trap door; possibly the same trap
   Blunt falls through a few lines later

LUCETTA.

> You know I was never guilty of that folly, my dear Phillippo, but with yourself — but come, let's see what we have got by this.

PHILLIPPO.

> A rich coat! Sword and hat — these breeches, too, are well lined — see here, a gold watch! A purse — ha! Gold! At least two hundred pistoles! A bunch of diamond rings! And one with the family arms! A gold box — with a medal of his king! And his lady mother's picture! These were sacred relics, believe me. See, the waistband of his breeches have a mine of gold! Old Queen Bess's, we have a quarrel to her ever since eighty-eight, and may therefore justify the theft; the Inquisition might have committed it.

LUCETTA.

> See, a bracelet of bowed [†] gold! These his sisters tied about his arm at parting — but well — for all this, I fear his being a stranger may make a noise and hinder our trade with them hereafter.

PHILLIPPO.

> That's our security; he is not only a stranger to us, but to the country too — the common shore[†] into which he is descended, thou knowst conducts him into another street, which this light will hinder him from ever finding again — he knows neither your name, nor that of the street where your house is, nay nor the way to his own lodgings.

LUCETTA.

> And art not thou an unmerciful rogue! Not to afford him one night for all this? I should not have been such a Jew.

---

41 old Queen Bess] Queen Elizabeth I, who reigned from 1558-1603

42 eighty-eight] In 1588 the Spanish Armada advanced towards England. In England the Armada was seen as a triumph of English sea-power, although a storm wrecked and dispersed many of the Spanish galleons.

45 bowed] bent, braided (?)

49 common shore] sewer

PHILLIPPO.

Blame me not, Lucetta, to keep as much of thee as I can to myself — come, that thought makes me wanton! Let's to bed! Sancho, lock up these.
This is the fleece which fools do bear
Designed for witty men to shear. 60

Exeunt.

Scene IV

The scene changes and discovers Blunt, creeping out of a common shore, his
face, etc. all dirty.

BLUNT.

Oh lord!

Climbing up.

I am got out at last, and (which is a miracle) without a clue — and
now to damning and cursing — but if that would ease me, where
shall I begin? With my fortune, myself, or the quean that cozened
me? What a dog was I to believe in woman! Oh coxcomb! Igno- 5
rant conceited coxcomb! To fancy she could be enamoured with
my person! At first sight enamoured! Oh, I'm a cursed puppy!
'Tis plain, "fool" was writ upon my forehead! She perceived it —
saw the Essex calf there — for what allurements could there be in
this countenance, which I can endure, because I'm acquainted 10
with it — oh, dull silly dog! To be thus soothed into a cozening!
Had I been drunk, I might fondly have credited the young
quean! But as I was in my right wits, to be thus cheated confirms
it I am a dull, believing, English country fop — but my comrades!
Death and the devil! There's the worst of all — then a ballad will 15
be sung tomorrow on the prado, to a lousy tune of "The Enchanted 'Squire, and the Annihilated Damsel" — but Frederick,

---

2 clue] ball of thread used as a guide out of a maze; also "clew"
4 quean] prostitute
16 prado] field, lawn, meadow (Sp.)

that rogue, and the colonel, will abuse me beyond all Christian
patience — had she left me my clothes, I have a bill of exchange
at home would have saved my credit — but now all hope is taken   20
from me — well, I'll home (if I can find the way) with this consola-
tion, that I am not the first kind, believing coxcomb; but there
are, gallants, many such good natures amongst ye.
And though you've better arts to hide your follies,
Adsheartlikins y'are all as errant cullies.   25

Exit.[†]

Scene V, the Garden in the Night   I

Enter Florinda in an undress, with a key and a little box.

FLORINDA.

Well, thus far I'm on my way to happiness. I have got myself free
from Callis; my brother too, I find by yonder light, is got into his
cabinet, and thinks not of me; I have by good fortune got the key
of the garden back-door. I'll open it to prevent Belvile's knocking
— a little noise will now alarm my brother. Now am I as fearful as   5
a young thief.

Unlocks the door.

Hark — what noise is that? Oh, 'twas the wind that played
amongst the boughs — Belvile stays long, methinks — it's time —
stay — for fear of a surprise, I'll hide these jewels in yonder jes-
samin..   10

She goes to lay down the box.

---

25 cullies] fools; dupes
Stage Direction: undress] casual dress or robe worn at home
3 cabinet] small private room
9 jessamin] jasmine

Enter Willmore drunk.

WILLMORE.

What the devil is become of these fellows, Belvile and Frederick?
They promised to stay at the next corner for me, but who the
devil knows the corner of a full moon — now — whereabouts am
I? Hah — what have we here, a garden! A very convenient place
to sleep in — hah — what has God sent us here! A female! By this   15
light a woman! I'm a dog if it be not a very wench!

FLORINDA.

He's come! Hah — who's there?

WILLMORE.

Sweet soul! Let me salute thy shoe-string.

FLORINDA.

'Tis not my Belvile — good heavens! I know him not — who are
you, and from whence come you?   20

WILLMORE.

Prithee — prithee child — not so many questions — let it suffice I
am here, child — come, come kiss me.

FLORINDA.

Good gods! What luck is mine?

WILLMORE.

Only good luck, child, parlous good luck — come hither — 'tis a
delicate shining wench — by this hand she's perfumed, and smells   25
like any nosegay — prithee, dear soul, let's not play the fool, and
lose time — precious time — for as gad shall save me, I'm as honest a fellow as breathes, though I'm a little disguised at present —
come I say. Why, thou may'st be free with me, I'll be very secret.
I'll not boast who 'twas obliged me, not I — for hang me if I know   30
thy name.

FLORINDA.

Heavens! What a filthy beast is this?

WILLMORE.

I am so, and thou ought'st the sooner to lie with me for that reason — for look you child, there will be no sin in't, because 'twas
neither designed nor premeditated. 'Tis pure accident on both   35

---

24 parlous] extremely
28 disguised] drunk

sides — that's a certain thing now. Indeed should I make love to you, and you vow fidelity — and swear and lie till you believed and yielded — that were to make it wilful fornication, the crying sin of the nation. Thou art therefore (as thou art a good Christian) obliged in conscience to deny me nothing. Now — come be kind without any more idle prating.

FLORINDA.

Oh I am ruined — wicked man, unhand me.

WILLMORE.

Wicked! Egad child, a judge, were he young and vigorous and saw those eyes of thine, would know 'twas they gave the first blow — the first provocation — come prithee, let's lose no time, I say — this is a fine convenient place.

FLORINDA.

Sir, let me go, I conjure you, or I'll call out.

WILLMORE.

Ay, ay, you were best to call witness to see how finely you treat me — do —

FLORINDA.

I'll cry murder, rape, or anything if you do not instantly let me go.

WILLMORE.

A rape! Come, come, you lie, you baggage, you lie. What, I'll warrant you would fain have the world believe now that you are not so forward as I. No, not you. Why, at this time of night, was your cobweb door set open, dear spider — but to catch flies? Hah — come — or I shall be damnably angry. Why, what a coil is here —

FLORINDA.

Sir, can you think —

WILLMORE.

That you would do't for nothing — oh, oh, I find what you would be at — look here's a pistole[†] for you — here's a work indeed — here — take it I say —

FLORINDA.

For heavens sake, sir, as you're a gentleman —

---

55 coil] turmoil, fuss

WILLMORE.

So — now — now — she would be wheedling me for more — what,
you will not take it then — you are resolved you will not — come —
come take it or I'll put it up again — for look ye, I never give
more. Why how now, mistress, are you so high i'th'mouth a pistole[†] won't down with you — hah — why, what a works here — in   65
good time — come, no struggling to be gone — but an y'are good
at a dumb wrestle I'm for ye — look ye — I'm for ye —

She struggles with him.

Enter Belvile and Frederick.

BELVILE.

The door is open. A pox of this mad fellow; I'm angry that we've
lost him; I durst have sworn he had followed us.

FREDERICK.

But you were so hasty, colonel to be gone.   70

FLORINDA.

Help! Help! Murder! Help — oh, I am ruined.

BELVILE.

Ha! Sure that's Florinda's voice.

Comes up to them.

A man! Villain, let go that lady!

A noise. Willmore turns and draws, Frederick interposes.

FLORINDA.

Belvile! Heavens! My brother too is coming, and 'twill be impossible to escape — Belvile, I conjure you to walk under my chamber   75
window, from whence I'll give you some instructions what to do
— this rude man has undone us.

Exit.

---

66 an] if

WILLMORE.

Belvile!

Enter Pedro, Stephano, and other servants with lights.

PEDRO.

I'm betrayed! Run, Stephano, and see if Florinda be safe.

Exit Stephano.

So, whoe'er they be, all is not well. I'll to Florinda's chamber.

They fight and Pedro's party beats 'em out. Going out, meets Stephano.

STEPHANO.

You need not, sir; the poor lady's fast asleep and thinks no harm. I would not awake her sir, for fear of frighting her with your danger.

PEDRO.

I'm glad she's there — rascals, how came the garden door open?

STEPHANO.

That question comes too late, sir; some of my fellow servants masquerading, I'll warrant.

PEDRO.

Masquerading! A lewd custom to debauch our youth — there's something more in this then, I imagine.

Exeunt.

Scene VI

Scene changes to the street.

Enter Belvile in rage, Frederick holding him, and Willmore melancholy.

WILLMORE.

Why, how the devil should I know Florinda?

BELVILE.

A plague of your ignorance! If it had not been Florinda, must you be a beast? A brute? A senseless swine?

WILLMORE.

Well, sir, you see I am endued with patience — I can bear —
though egad, y'are very free with me, methinks. I was in good 5
hopes the quarrel would have been on my side, for so uncivilly
interrupting me.

BELVILE.

Peace, brute! Whilst thou'rt safe — oh, I'm distracted.

WILLMORE.

Nay, nay, I'm an unlucky dog, that's certain.

BELVILE.

Ah, curse upon the star that ruled my birth! Or whatsoever other 10
influence that makes me still so wretched.

WILLMORE.

Thou break'st my heart with these complaints. There is no star in
fault, no influence but sack, the cursed sack I drunk.

FREDERICK.

Why how the devil came you so drunk?

WILLMORE.

Why how the devil came you so sober? 15

BELVILE.

A curse upon his thin skull, he was always before hand that way.

FREDERICK.

Prithee, dear colonel, forgive him, he's sorry for his fault.

BELVILE.

He's always so after he has done a mischief — a plague on all such
brutes.

WILLMORE.

By this light, I took her for an errant harlot. 20

BELVILE.

Damn your debauched opinion! Tell me sot, had'st thou so much
sense and light about thee to distinguish her woman, and
could'st not see something about her face and person, to strike
an awful reverence into thy soul?

WILLMORE.

Faith no, I considered her as mere a woman as I could wish. 25

BELVILE.

'Sdeath, I have no patience — draw, or I'll kill you.

---

4 endued] equipped, supplied

WILLMORE.

Let that alone till tomorrow, and if I set not all right again, use your pleasure.

BELVILE.

Tomorrow! Damn it.

The spiteful[†] light will lead me to no happiness.

Tomorrow is Antonio's, and perhaps

Guides him to my undoing — oh, that I could meet

This rival! This pow'rful fortunate!

WILLMORE.

What then?

BELVILE.

Let thy own reason, or my rage, instruct thee.

WILLMORE.

I shall be finely informed then, no doubt; hear me, colonel — hear me — show me the man and I'll do his business.

BELVILE.

I know him no more than thou, or if I did I should not need thy aid.

WILLMORE.

This, you say, is Angellica's house. I promised the kind baggage to lie with her tonight.

Offers to go in.

Enter Antonio and his page. Antonio knocks on the hilt of's sword.

ANTONIO.

You paid the thousand crowns I directed?

PAGE.

To the lady's old woman, sir, I did.

WILLMORE.

Who the devil have we here!

BELVILE.

I'll now plant myself under Florinda's window, and if I find no comfort there, I'll die.

Exeunt Belvile and Frederick.

Enter Moretta.

MORETTA.

    Page!

PAGE.

    Here's my lord.

WILLMORE.

    How is this! A picaroon going to board my frigate? Here's one
chase gun for you.   50

Drawing his sword, justles Antonio who turns and draws. They fight,
Antonio falls.

MORETTA.

    Oh bless us! We're all undone!

Runs in and shuts the door.

PAGE.

    Help! Murder!

Belvile returns at the noise of the fighting.

BELVILE.

    Ha! The mad rogue's engaged in some unlucky adventure again.

Enter two or three masqueraders.

MASQUERADERS.

    Ha! A man killed!

WILLMORE.

    How! A man killed! Then I'll go home to sleep.   55

Puts up and reels out. Exeunt masqueraders another way.

BELVILE.

    Who should it be! Pray heaven the rogue is safe, for all my quar-
rel to him.

Stage Direction: justles] jostles

As Belvile is groping about, enter an officer and six soldiers.

SOLDIER.
Who's there?

OFFICER.
So here's one dispatched — secure the murderer.

Soldiers seize on Belvile.

BELVILE.
Do not mistake my charity for murder!
I came to his assistance.

OFFICER.
That shall be tried, sir — St. Jago, swords drawn in carnival time!

Goes to Antonio.

ANTONIO.
Thy hand, prithee.

OFFICER.
Ha! Don Antonio! Look well to the villain there. How is it, sir?

ANTONIO.
I'm hurt.

BELVILE.
Has my humanity made me a criminal?

OFFICER.
Away with him.

BELVILE.
What a cursed chance is this?

Exeunt soldiers with Belvile.

ANTONIO.   [*To the officer.*]
This is the man that has set upon me twice — carry him to my apartment, till you have farther orders from me.

Exit Antonio led.

---

62 St. Jago] St. James the Apostle

ACT IV.
Scene I. A fine room.

Discovers Belvile as by dark alone.

BELVILE.

When shall I be weary of railing on fortune, who is resolved
never to turn with smiles upon me? Two such defeats in one
night — none but the devil and that mad rogue could have con-
trived to have plagued me with. I am here a prisoner — but where
— heaven knows — and if there be murder done, I can soon de-   5
cide the fate of a stranger in a nation without mercy. Yet this is
nothing to the torture my soul bows with when I think of losing
my fair, my dear, Florinda — hark — my door opens — a light — a
man — and seems of quality — armed too! Now shall I die like a
dog without defence.   10

*Enter Antonio in a nightgown with a light; his arm in a scarf, and a sword
under his arm. He sets the candle on the table.*

ANTONIO.

Sir, I come to know what injuries I have done you that could pro-
voke you to so mean an action as to attack me basely, without al-
lowing time for my defence?

BELVILE.

Sir, for a man in my circumstances to plead innocence would
look like fear — but view me well, and you will find no marks of   15
coward on me; nor anything that betrays that brutality you ac-
cuse me with.

ANTONIO.

In vain, sir, you impose upon my sense.
You are not only he who drew on me last night,
But yesterday before the same house, that of Angellica.   20
Yet there is something in your face and mien
That makes me wish I were mistaken.

Stage Direction: nightgown] robe, dressing gown
21 mien] appearance, look

BELVILE.

I own I fought today in the defence of a friend of mine, with
whom you (if you're the same) and your party were first engaged.
Perhaps you think this crime enough to kill me,   2
But if you do, I cannot fear you'll do it basely.

ANTONIO.

No, sir, I'll make you fit for a defence with this.

Gives him the sword.

BELVILE.

This gallantry surprises me — nor know I how to use this present,
sir, against a man so brave.

ANTONIO.

You shall not need.   3
For know, I come to snatch you from a danger
That is decreed against you;
Perhaps your life, or long imprisonment;
And 'twas with so much courage you offended,
I cannot see you punished.   3

BELVILE.

How shall I pay this generosity?

ANTONIO.

It had been safer to have killed another
Than have attempted me.
To show your danger, sir, I'll let you know my quality;
And 'tis the viceroy's son whom you have wounded.   4

BELVILE. [*Aside.*]

The viceroy's son!
Death and confusion! Was this plague reserved
To complete all the rest? Obliged by him!
The man of all the world I would destroy.

ANTONIO.

You seem disordered, sir.   4

BELVILE.

Yes, trust me sir, I am, and 'tis with pain
That man receives such bounties,
Who wants the pow'r to pay 'em back again.

ANTONIO.

To gallant spirits 'tis indeed uneasy;
But you may quickly overpay me, sir.   5

BELVILE.

Then I am well.

[*Aside.*] Kind heav'n, but set us even,

That I may fight with him and keep my honour safe.

— Oh, I'm impatient, sir, to be discounting the mighty debt I owe

you; command me quickly —   55

ANTONIO.

I have a quarrel with a rival, sir,

About the maid we love.

BELVILE.   [*Aside.*]

Death, 'tis Florinda he means —

That thought destroys my reason,

And I shall kill him —   60

ANTONIO.

My rival, sir,

Is one has all the virtues man can boast of.

BELVILE. [*Aside.*]

Death! Who should this be?

ANTONIO.†

He challenged me to meet him on the Molo

As soon as day appeared; but last night's quarrel   65

Has made my arm unfit to guide a sword.

BELVILE.

I apprehend you, sir; you'd have me kill the man

That lays a claim to the maid you speak of.

I'll do't — I'll fly to do't!

ANTONIO.

Sir, do you know her?   70

BELVILE.

No, sir, but 'tis enough she is admired by you.

ANTONIO.

Sir, I shall rob you of the glory on't,

For you must fight under my name and dress.

BELVILE.

That opinion must be strangely obliging that makes

You think I can personate the brave Antonio,   75

Whom I can but strive to imitate.

ANTONIO.

You say too much to my advantage.

Come, sir, the day appears that calls you forth.

Within, sir, is the habit.

Exit Antonio.

BELVILE.

Fantastic fortune, thou deceitful light,   80
That cheats the wearied traveller by night,
Though on a precipice each step you tread,
I am resolved to follow where you lead.

Exit.

Scene II, The Molo.   IV

Enter Florinda and Callis in masks with Stephano.

FLORINDA. [*Aside.*]

I'm dying with my fears; Belvile's not coming as I expected under
my window, makes me believe that all those fears are true.
— Canst thou not tell with whom my brother fights?

STEPHANO.

No, madam, they were both in masquerade. I was by when they
challenged one another, and they had decided the quarrel then,   5
but were prevented by some cavaliers, which made 'em put it off
till now — but I am sure 'tis about you they fight.

FLORINDA. [*Aside.*]

Nay, then 'tis with Belvile, for what other lover have I that dares
fight for me, except Antonio? And he is too much in favour with
my brother. If it be he, for whom shall I direct my prayers to   10
heaven?

STEPHANO.

Madam, I must leave you, for if my master see me, I shall be
hanged for being your conductor. I† escaped narrowly for the excuse I made for you last night i'th'garden.

FLORINDA.

And I'll reward thee for't — prithee no more.   15

Exit Stephano.

Enter Don Pedro in his masquing habit.

PEDRO.

    Antonio's late today; the place will fill, and we may be prevented.

Walks about.

FLORINDA.   [*Aside.*]

    "Antonio" — sure I heard amiss.

PEDRO.

    But who will not excuse a happy lover

    When soft fair arms confine the yielding neck,

    And the kind whisper languishingly breathes,   20

    "Must you begone so soon?"

    Sure I had dwelt for ever on her bosom.

    But stay, he's here.

Enter Belvile dressed in Antonio's clothes.

FLORINDA.

    'Tis not Belvile; half my fears are vanisht.

PEDRO.

    Antonio!   25

BELVILE.   [*Aside.*]

    This must be he.

    — You're early, sir — I do not use to be outdone this way.

PEDRO.

    The wretched, sir, are watchful, and 'tis enough

    You've the advantage of me in Angellica.

BELVILE.   [*Aside.*]

    Angellica! Or I've mistook my man or else Antonio.   30

    Can he forget his interest in Florinda,

    And fight for common prize?

PEDRO.

    Come, sir, you know our terms —

BELVILE.   [*Aside.*]

    By heav'n not I.

    — No talking, I am ready, sir.   35

Offers to fight, Florinda runs in.

FLORINDA.   [*To Belvile.*]

    Oh hold! Whoe'er you be, I do conjure you hold!

If you strike here — I die.

PEDRO.

Florinda!

BELVILE.

Florinda imploring for my rival!

PEDRO.

Away, this kindness is unreasonable.   4

Puts her by; they fight; she runs in just as Belvile disarms Pedro.

FLORINDA.

Who are you, sir, that dares deny my prayers?

BELVILE.

Thy prayers destroy him; if thou would'st preserve him,
Do that thou'rt unacquainted with and curse him.

She holds him.

FLORINDA.

By all you hold most dear, by her you love,
I do conjure you, touch him not.   4

BELVILE.

By her I love!
See — I obey — and at your feet resign
The useless trophy of my victory.

Lays his sword at her feet.

PEDRO.

Antonio, you've done enough to prove you love Florinda.

BELVILE.

Love Florinda!   5
Does heav'n love adoration, prayer or penitence! Love her! Here,
sir — your sword again.

Snatches up the sword and gives it him.

Upon this truth I'll fight my life away.

PEDRO.

No, you've redeemed my sister, and my friendship!

*He gives him Florinda and pulls off his vizard to show his face and puts it
on again.*

BELVILE.

    Don Pedro! 55

PEDRO.

    Can you resign your claims to other women,

    And give your heart entirely to Florinda?

BELVILE.

    Entire as dying saints' confessions are.

    I can delay my happiness no longer.

    This minute let me make Florinda mine! 60

PEDRO.

    This minute let it be — no time so proper.

    This night my father will arrive from Rome,

    And possibly may hinder what we purpose!

FLORINDA.

    Oh heavens! This minute!

Enter masqueraders and pass over.

BELVILE.

    Oh, do not ruin me! 65

PEDRO.

    The place begins to fill, and that we may not be observed, do you
walk off to St. Peter's church, where I will meet you, and conclude your happiness.

BELVILE.

    I'll meet you there.

    [*Aside.*] — If there be no more saints' churches in Naples. 70

FLORINDA.

    Oh, stay sir, and recall your hasty doom!

    Alas, I have not yet prepared my heart

    To entertain so strange a guest.

PEDRO.

    Away, this silly modesty is assumed too late.

BELVILE.

    Heaven, madam! What do you do? 75

FLORINDA.

    Do! Despise the man that lays a tyrant's claim

    To what he ought to conquer by submission.

BELVILE.

You do not know me — move a little this way.

Draws her aside.

FLORINDA.

Yes, you may force me even to the altar,
But not the holy man that offers there   80
Shall force me to be thine.

Pedro talks to Callis this while.

BELVILE.

Oh do not lose[†] so blest an opportunity —
See — 'tis your Belvile — not Antonio,
Whom your mistaken scorn and anger ruins.

Pulls off his vizard.

FLORINDA.

Belvile!   85
Where was my soul it could not meet thy voice
And take this knowledge in?

As they are talking, enter Willmore, finely dressed, and Frederick.

WILLMORE.

No intelligence, no news of Belvile yet — well, I am the most unlucky rascal in nature — ha — am I deceived? Or is it he? Look
Fred — 'tis he — my dear Belvile!   90

Runs and embraces him. Belvile's vizard falls out on's hand.

BELVILE.

Hell and confusion seize thee!

PEDRO.

Ha! Belvile! I beg your pardon sir.

Takes Florinda from him.

BELVILE.
    Nay, touch her not. She's mine by conquest, sir;
    I won her by my sword.
WILLMORE.
    Did'st thou so — and egad, child, we'll keep her by the sword.   95

Draws on Pedro. Belvile goes between.

BELVILE.
    Stand off!
    Thou'rt so profanely lewd, so curst by heaven,
    All quarrels thou espousest must be fatal.
WILLMORE.
    Nay, an you be so hot, my valour's coy, and shall be courted
    when you want it next.   100

Puts up his sword.

BELVILE.   [*To Pedro.*]
    You know I ought to claim a victor's right.
    But you're the brother to divine Florinda,
    To whom I'm such a slave — to purchase her,
    I durst not hurt the man she holds so dear.
PEDRO.
    'Twas by Antonio's, not by Belvile's sword   105
    This question should have been decided, sir.
    I must confess, much to your bravery's due,
    Both now, and when I met you last in arms.
    But I am nicely punctual in my word,
    As men of honour ought, and beg your pardon.   110
    For this mistake another time shall clear.

Aside to Florinda as they are going out.

    This was some plot between you and Belvile.
    But I'll prevent you.

Belvile looks after her and begins to walk up and down in rage.

WILLMORE.

　Do not be modest now and lose[†] the woman, but if we shall fetch
　her back so —   115

BELVILE.

　Do not speak to me —

WILLMORE.

　Not speak to you — egad, I'll speak to you, and will be answered,
　too.

BELVILE.

　Will you, sir —

WILLMORE.

　I know I've done some mischief, but I'm so dull a puppy, that I'm   120
　the son of a whore if I know how, or where — prithee inform my
　understanding —

BELVILE.

　Leave me, I say, and leave me instantly.

WILLMORE.

　I will not leave you in this humour, nor till I know my crime.

BELVILE.

　Death, I'll tell you sir —   125

Draws and runs at Willmore. He runs out, Belvile after him;
Frederick interposes.

Enter Angellica, Moretta and Sebastian.

ANGELLICA.

　Ha — Sebastian —
　Is not that Willmore? Haste[†] — haste and bring him back.

FREDERICK.

　The colonel's mad — I never saw him thus before. I'll after 'em
　lest he do some mischief, for I am sure Willmore will not draw
　on him.   130

Exit.

ANGELLICA.

　I am all rage! My first desires defeated!
　For one for aught[†] he knows that has no
　Other merit than her quality,
　Her being Don Pedro's sister — he loves her!

I know 'tis so — dull, dull, insensible — 135
He will not see me now though oft invited,
And broke his word last night — false perjured man!
He that but yesterday fought for my favours,
And would have made his life a sacrifice
To've gained one night with me, 140
Must now be hired and courted to my arms.

MORETTA.

I told you what would come on't, but Moretta's an old doting
fool. Why did you give him five hundred crowns, but to set himself out for other lovers? You should have kept him poor if you
had meant to have had any good from him. 145

ANGELLICA.

Oh, name not such mean trifles — had I given him all
My youth has earned from sin,
I had not lost a thought, nor sigh upon't.
But I have given him my eternal rest,
My whole repose, my future joys, my heart! 150
My virgin heart, Moretta! Oh, 'tis gone!

MORETTA.

Curse on him, here he comes;
How fine she has made him too.

Enter Willmore and Sebastian; Angellica turns and walks away.

WILLMORE.

How now, turned shadow!
Fly when I pursue and follow when I fly! 155

Sings.

Stay, gentle shadow of my dove
And tell me ere I go,
Whether the substance may not prove
A fleeting thing like you.

There's a soft kind look remaining yet. 160

As she turns she looks on him.

ANGELLICA.

Well sir, you may be gay; all happiness, all joys, pursue you still. Fortune's your slave, and gives you every hour choice of new hearts and beauties, till you are cloyed with the repeated bliss which others vainly languish for.

[*Aside*]‡ But know, false man, that I shall be revenged.   1⁰

Turns away in rage.

WILLMORE.

So, gad, there are of those faint-hearted lovers, whom such a sharp lesson next their hearts would make as impotent as four-score. Pox o' this whining. My business is to laugh and love. A pox on't — I hate your sullen lover. A man shall lose as much time to put you in humour now, as would serve to gain a new   1⁷ woman.

ANGELLICA.

I scorn to cool that fire I cannot raise,
Or do the drudgery of your virtuous mistress.

WILLMORE.

A virtuous mistress! Death, what a thing thou hast found out for me. Why, what the devil should I do with a virtuous woman? A   1⁷ sort of ill-natured creatures, that take a pride to torment a lover. Virtue is but an infirmity in woman, a disease that renders even the handsome ungrateful; whilst the ill-favoured, for want of so-licitations and address, only fancy themselves so. I have lain with a woman of quality, who has all the while been railing at whores.   18

ANGELLICA.

I will not answer for your mistress's virtue,
Though she be young enough to know no guilt;
And I could wish you would persuade my heart
'Twas the two hundred thousand crowns you courted.

WILLMORE.

Two hundred thousand crowns! What story's this? What trick?   18 What woman? Ha!

ANGELLICA.

How strange you make it; have you forgot the creature you enter-tained on the piazza last night?

WILLMORE. [*Aside.*]

Ha! My gypsy worth two hundred thousand crowns! Oh, how I long to be with her — pox, I knew she was of quality.   .   1⁹

ANGELLICA.

    False man! I see my ruin in thy face.

    How many vows you breathed upon my bosom,

    Never to be unjust — have you forgot so soon?

WILLMORE.

    Faith no, I was just coming to repeat 'em — but here's a humour
indeed would make a man a saint. [*Aside.*] — Would she would   195
be angry enough to leave me, and command me not to wait on
her.

            Enter Hellena dressed in man's clothes.

HELLENA.   [*Aside*]

    This must be Angellica! I know it by her mumping matron here.
Ay, ay, 'tis she! My mad captain's with her too, for all his swear-
ing — how this unconstant humour makes me love him!   200
— Pray, good grave gentlewoman, is not this Angellica?

MORETTA.

    My too young sir, it is — [*Aside*]‡ I hope 'tis one from Don Anto-
nio.

               Goes to Angellica.

HELLENA.   [*Aside.*]

    Well, something I'll do to vex him for this.

ANGELLICA.

    I will not speak with him; am I in humour to receive a lover?

WILLMORE.

    Not speak with him! Why I'll be gone and wait your idler minutes —   205
can I show less obedience to the thing I love so fondly?

               Offers to go.

ANGELLICA.

    A fine excuse this! Stay —

---

198 mumping] mumbling, grimacing, sullen

WILLMORE.

    And hinder your advantage! Should I repay your bounties so un-
gratefully?

ANGELLICA.

    Come hither, boy — that I may let you see   210

    How much above[†] the advantages you name

    I prize one minute's joy with you.

WILLMORE.

    Oh, you destroy me with this endearment.

Impatient to be gone.

    Death! How shall I get away? Madam, 'twill not be fit I should be
seen with you — besides, it will not be convenient — and I've a   215
friend — that's dangerously sick.

ANGELLICA.

    I see you're impatient — yet you shall stay.

WILLMORE.   [*Aside, and walks about impatiently.*]

    And miss my assignation with my gypsy.

HELLENA.

    Madam,

Moretta brings Hellena, who addresses herself to Angellica.

    You'll hardly pardon my intrusion   220

    When you shall know my business,

    And I'm too young to tell my tale with art;

    But there must be a wondrous store of goodness,

    Where so much beauty dwells.

ANGELLICA.

    A pretty advocate, whoever sent thee.   225

    Prithee proceed — [*To Willmore, who is stealing off.*] — nay, sir, you
shall not go.

WILLMORE.   [*Aside.*]

    Then I shall lose my dear gypsy for ever — pox on't, she stays me
out of spite.

HELLENA.[†]

    I am related to a lady, madam,   230

    Young, rich, and nobly born, but has the fate

    To be in love with a young English gentleman.

    Strangely she loves him, at first sight she loved him,

But did adore him when she heard him speak;
For he, she said, had charms in every word,   235
That failed not to surprise, to wound and conquer.

WILLMORE.   [*Aside.*]

Ha! Egad, I hope this concerns me.

ANGELLICA.   [*Aside*]‡

'Tis my false man, he means — would he were gone.
This praise will raise his pride, and ruin me — [*To Willmore*]‡ Well
Since you are so impatient to be gone   240
I will release you, sir.

WILLMORE.   [*Aside.*]

Nay, then, I'm sure 'twas me he spoke of; this cannot be the effects of kindness in her.

— No, madam, I've considered better on't, and will not give you
cause of jealousy.   245

ANGELLICA.

But, sir, I've — business, that —

WILLMORE.

This shall not do; I know 'tis but to try me.

ANGELLICA.

Well, to your story, boy — [*Aside.*] though 'twill undo me.

HELLENA.

With this addition to his other beauties,
He won her unresisting tender heart.   250
He vowed, and sighed, and swore he loved her dearly;
And she believed the cunning flatterer,
And thought herself the happiest maid alive.
Today was the appointed time by both
To consummate their bliss,   255
The virgin, altar, and the priest were dressed
And whilst she languished for th'expected bridegroom,
She heard he paid his broken vows to you.

WILLMORE.

So, this is some dear rogue that's in love with me, and this way
lets me know it; or if it be not me, he† means someone whose   260
place I may supply.

ANGELLICA.

Now I perceive
The cause of thy impatience to be gone,
And all the business of this glorious dress.

WILLMORE.
    Damn the young prater, I know not what he means. 2(

HELLENA.
    Madam,
    In your fair eyes I read too much concern,
    To tell my farther business.

ANGELLICA.
    Prithee, sweet youth, talk on, thou mayest perhaps
    Raise here a storm that may undo my passion, 2?
    And then I'll grant thee anything.

HELLENA.
    Madam, 'tis to entreat you (oh unreasonable),
    You would not see this stranger;
    For if you do, she vows you are undone,
    Though nature never made a man so excellent, 2?
    And sure he'ad been a god, but for inconstancy.

WILLMORE.   [*Aside.*]
    Ah, rogue, how finely he's instructed!
    — 'Tis plain; some woman that has seen me *en passant.*

ANGELLICA.
    Oh, I shall burst with jealousy! Do you know the man you speak
    of? 2{

HELLENA.
    Yes, madam, he used to be in buff and scarlet.

ANGELLICA.   [*To Willmore.*]
    Thou, false as hell, what canst thou say to this?

WILLMORE.
    By heaven —

ANGELLICA.
    Hold, do not damn thyself —

HELLENA.
    Nor hope to be believed. 2{

                He walks about, they follow.

---

265 prater] one who prates; i.e. talks foolishly or irrelevantly
278 *en passant*] in passing

ANGELLICA.

Oh perjured man!

Is't thus you pay my generous passion back?

HELLENA.

Why would you, sir, abuse my lady's faith?

ANGELLICA.

And use me so unhumanely.

HELLENA.

A maid so young, so innocent —

WILLMORE.

Ah, young devil.†

ANGELLICA.

Dost thou know thy life is in† my power?

HELLENA.

Or think my lady cannot be revenged?

WILLMORE. [*Aside.*]

So, so, the storm comes finely on.

ANGELLICA.

Now thou art silent, guilt has struck thee dumb.

Oh, hadst thou still been so, I'd lived in safety.

She turns away and weeps.

WILLMORE. [*Aside to Hellena; looks toward Angellica to watch her turning and as she comes towards them he meets her.*]

Sweetheart, the lady's name and house — quickly, I'm impatient to be with her.

HELLENA. [*Aside.*]

So, now is he for another woman.

WILLMORE.

The impudentest† young thing in nature,

I cannot persuade him out of his error, madam.

ANGELLICA.

I know he's in the right — yet thou'st a tongue

That would persuade him to deny his faith.

In rage walks away.

WILLMORE.

Her name, her name, dear boy —

290

295

300

Said softly to Hellena.

HELLENA.

    Have you forgot it, sir?   30

WILLMORE.   [*Aside.*]

    Oh, I perceive he's not to know I am a stranger to this lady.

    — Yes, yes, I do know — but I have forgot the —

Angellica turns.

    — By heaven such early confidence I never saw.

ANGELLICA.

    Did I not charge you with this mistress, sir?

    Which you denied, though I beheld your perjury.   3

    This little generosity of thine, has rendered back my heart.

Walks away.

WILLMORE.

    So, you have made sweet work here, my little mischief; look your
lady be kind and good-natured now, or I shall have but a cursed
bargain on't.

Angellica turns toward them.

    — The rogue's bred up to mischief;   31

    Art thou so great a fool to credit him?

ANGELLICA.

    Yes, I do, and you in vain impose upon me.

    Come hither, boy — is not this he you spake of?

HELLENA.

    I think — it is; I cannot swear, but I vow he has just such another
lying lover's look.   32

Hellena looks in his face, he gazes on her.

WILLMORE.

    Hah! Do not I know that face —

    [*Aside.*] By heaven, my little gypsy; what a dull dog was I,

    Had I but looked that way I'd known her.

    Are all my hopes of a new woman banished?

— Egad, if I do not fit thee for this, hang me.   325
— Madam, I have found out the plot.

HELLENA.   [*Aside*]‡

Oh lord, what does he say? Am I discovered now?

WILLMORE.

Do you see this young spark here?

HELLENA.   [*Aside*]‡

He'll tell her who I am.

WILLMORE.

Who do you think this is?   330

HELLENA.   [*Aside*]‡

Ay, ay, he does know me —
Nay, dear captain! I am undone if you discover me.

WILLMORE.

Nay, nay, no cogging; she shall know what a precious mistress I
have.

HELLENA.

Will you be such a devil?   335

WILLMORE.   [*Aside.*] ‡

Nay, nay, I'll teach you to spoil sport you will not make.
— This small ambassador comes not from a person of quality as
you imagine, and he says, but from a very errant gypsy, the talk-
ingest, pratingest, cantingest little animal thou ever saw'st.

ANGELLICA.

What news you tell me, that's the thing I mean.   340

HELLENA.   [*Aside.*]

Would I were well off the place; if ever I go a captain-hunting
again —

WILLMORE.

Mean that thing? That gypsy thing? Thou may'st as well be jealous of thy monkey or parrot, as of her; a German motion were
worth a dozen of her, and a dream were a better enjoyment, a   345
creature of a constitution fitter for heaven than man.

HELLENA.   [*Aside.*]

Though I'm sure he lies, yet this vexes me.

---

325 fit] pay back
333 cogging] wheedling, begging
344 motion] puppet

ANGELLICA.

> You are mistaken, she's a Spanish woman
> Made up of no such dull materials.

WILLMORE.

> Materials, egad an thee be made of any that will either dispense   35
> or admit of love, I'll be bound to continence.

HELLENA.   [*Aside to him.*]

> Unreasonable man, do you think so?

WILLMORE.†

> You may return, my little brazen head, and tell your lady that till
> she be handsome enough to be beloved, or I dull enough to be
> religious, there will be small hopes of me.   35

ANGELLICA.

> Did you not promise then to marry her?

WILLMORE.

> Not I, by heaven.

ANGELLICA.

> You cannot undeceive my fears and torments, till you have
> vowed you will not marry her.

HELLENA.   [*Aside.*]

> If he swears that, he'll be revenged on me indeed for all my   36
> rogueries.

ANGELLICA.

> I know what arguments you'll bring up against me — fortune, and
> honour —

WILLMORE.

> Honour, I tell you, I hate it in your sex, and those that fancy
> themselves possessed of that foppery are the most impertinently   36
> troublesome of all womankind, and will transgress nine com-
> mandments to keep one, and to satisfy your jealousy, I swear.

HELLENA.   [*Aside to him.*]

> Oh, no swearing, dear captain.

WILLMORE.

> If it were possible I should ever be inclined to marry, it should be
> some kind young sinner, one that has generosity enough to give   37
> a favour handsomely to one that can ask it discreetly, one that

---

353 brazen head] a brazen (brass) head which can speak or prophesy

has wit enough to manage an intrigue of love – oh, how civil
such a wench is, to a man that does her the honour to marry her.

ANGELLICA.

By heaven, there's no faith in anything he says.

Enter Sebastian.

SEBASTIAN.

Madam, Don Antonio –   375

ANGELLICA.

Come hither.

HELLENA.   [*Aside*]‡

Ha! Antonio! He may be coming hither and he'll certainly discover me; I'll therefore retire without a ceremony.

Exit Hellena.

ANGELLICA.

I'll see him; get my coach ready.

SEBASTIAN.

It waits you, madam.   380

WILLMORE.

This is lucky. What, madam, now I may be gone and leave you to
the enjoyment of my rival?

ANGELLICA.

Dull man, that can'st not see how ill, how poor,
That false dissimulation looks – begone,
And never let me see thy cozening face again,   385
Lest I relapse and kill thee.

WILLMORE.

Yes, you can spare me now – farewell, till you're in better hu-
mour – I'm glad of this release –
[*Aside*]‡ Now for my gypsy:
For though to worse we change, yet still we find   390
New joys, new charms, in a new miss that's kind.

Exit Willmore.

ANGELLICA.

He's gone, and in this ague of my soul,
The shivering fit returns;

Oh, with what willing haste he took his leave,
As if the longed-for minute were arrived
Of some blest assignation.
In vain I have consulted all my charms,
In vain this beauty prized, in vain believed
My eyes could kindle any lasting fires.
I had forgot my name, my infamy,
And the reproach that honour lays on those
That dare pretend a sober passion here.
Nice reputation, though it leave behind
More virtues than inhabit where that dwells,
Yet that once gone, those virtues shine no more.
Then since I am not fit to be beloved,
I am resolved to think on a revenge
On him that soothed me thus to my undoing.

Exeunt.

Scene III: A Street.

*Enter Florinda and Valeria in habits different from that
they have been seen in.*

FLORINDA.
We're happily escaped, and yet I tremble still.

VALERIA.
Lover, and fear! Why, I am but half an one, and yet I have courage for any attempt. Would Hellena were here, I would fain have
had her as deep in this mischief as we; she'll fare but ill else, I
doubt.

FLORINDA.
She pretended a visit to the Augustine nuns, but I believe some
other design carried her out; pray heaven we light on her.
Prithee what did'st do with Callis?

---

7 Augustine nuns] nuns of the order of St. Augustine

VALERIA.

When I saw no reason would do good on her, I followed her into
the wardrobe, and as she was looking for something in a great   10
chest, I toppled her in by the heels, snatched the key of the apartment where you were confined, locked her in, and left her bawl-
ing for help.

FLORINDA.

'Tis well you resolve to follow my fortunes, for thou darest never
appear at home again after such an action.   15

VALERIA.

That's according as the young stranger and I shall agree. But to
our business — I delivered your letter, your note† to Belvile, when
I got out under pretence of going to mass. I found him at his
lodging, and believe me it came seasonably, for never was a man
in so desperate a condition. I told him of your resolution of mak-   20
ing your escape today if your brother would be absent long
enough to permit you; if not, to die rather than be Antonio's.

FLORINDA.

Thou should'st have told him I was confined to my chamber
upon my brother's suspicion that the business on the Molo was a
plot laid between him and I.   25

VALERIA.

I said all this, and told him your brother was now gone to his de-
votions, and he resolves to visit every church till he find him; and
not only undeceive him in that, but caress him so as shall delay
his return home.

FLORINDA.

Oh heavens! He's here, and Belvile with him too.   30

They put on their vizards.

*Enter Don Pedro, Belvile, Willmore; Belvile and Don Pedro seeming in
serious discourse.*

VALERIA.

Walk boldly by them, and I'll come at distance, lest he suspect us.

She walks by them, and looks back on them.

WILLMORE.

Hah! A woman, and of an excellent mien.

PEDRO.

She throws a kind look back on you.

WILLMORE.

Death, 'tis a likely wench, and that kind look shall not be cast away — I'll follow her.   38

BELVILE.

Prithee do not.

WILLMORE.

Do not; by heavens, to the antipodes with such an invitation.

She goes out, and Willmore follows her.

BELVILE.

'Tis a mad fellow for a wench.

Enter Frederick.

FREDERICK.

Oh colonel, such news!

BELVILE.

Prithee, what?   40

FREDERICK.

News that will make you laugh in spite of fortune.

BELVILE.

What, Blunt has had some damned trick put upon him — cheated, banged or clapped?

FREDERICK.

Cheated sir, rarely cheated of all but his shirt and drawers. The unconscionable whore, too, turned him out before consumma-   45
tion, so that traversing the streets at midnight, the watch found him in this fresco, and conducted him home. By heaven, 'tis such a sight, and yet I durst as well been hanged as laugh at him or pity him; he beats all that do but ask him a question, and is in such an humour.   50

---

38 antipodes] the other side of the earth
43 banged] beaten
43 clapped] hit, struck; also, to get the clap (venereal disease)

PEDRO.

Who is't has met with this ill usage, sir?

BELVILE.

A friend of ours whom you must see for mirth's sake.

[*Aside.*] I'll employ him to give Florinda time for an escape.

PEDRO.

What is he?

BELVILE.

A young countryman of ours, one that has been educated at so 55
plentiful a rate, he yet ne'er knew the want of money, and 'twill
be a great jest to see how simply he'll look without it. For my
part, I'll lend him none, and the rogue know not how to put on a
borrowing face, and ask first; I'll let him see how good 'tis to play
our parts while I play his — prithee Frederick, do you go home 60
and keep him in that posture till we come.

Exeunt.

Enter Florinda from the farther end of the scene, looking behind her.

FLORINDA.

I am followed still — hah — my brother too, advancing this way.
Good heavens, defend me from being seen by him.

She goes off.

Enter Willmore, and after him Valeria, at a little distance.

WILLMORE.

Ah! There she sails; she looks back as she were willing to be
boarded. I'll warrant her prize. 65

He goes out, Valeria following.

Enter Hellena, just as he goes out, with a page.

---

65 sails...boarded...prize] In sea battles and piracy, captured ships, called prizes, were
seized as the property of those who boarded them.

HELLENA.

>Hah, is not that my captain that has a woman in chase? 'Tis not Angellica. Boy, follow those people at a distance, and bring me an account where they go in — I'll find his haunts, and plague him everywhere — ha — my brother —

Exit page; Belvile, Willmore, Pedro cross the stage; Hellena runs off.

Scene IV

Scene changes to another street. Enter Florinda.

FLORINDA.

>What shall I do, my brother now pursues me;
>Will no kind power protect me from his tyranny?
>Hah, here's a door open; I'll venture in, since nothing can be worse than to fall into his hands. My life and honour are at stake, and my necessity has no choice.

She goes in.
Enter Valeria and Hellena's page peeping after Florinda.

PAGE.

>Here she went in; I shall remember this house.

Exit Boy.

VALERIA.

>This is Belvile's lodging; she's gone in as readily as if she knew it — hah — here's that mad fellow again. I dare not venture in — I'll watch my opportunity.

Goes aside.
Enter Willmore, gazing about him.

WILLMORE.

>I have lost her hereabouts. Pox on't, she must not scape me so.

Goes out.

Scene V

Scene changes to Blunt's chamber; discovers him sitting on a couch in his shirt and drawers, reading.

BLUNT.

So, now my mind's a little at peace, since I have resolved revenge — a pox on this tailor though, for not bringing home the clothes I bespoke; and a pox of all poor cavaliers; a man can never keep a spare suit for 'em; and I shall have these rogues come in and find me naked, and then I'm undone. But I'm resolved to arm myself — the rascals shall not insult over me too much.

Puts on an old rusty sword, and buff belt.

Now, how like a morris dancer I am equipped — a fine lady-like whore to cheat me thus, without affording me a kindness for my money. A pox light on her, I shall never be reconciled to the sex more; she has made me as faithless as a physician, as uncharitable as a churchman, and as ill-natured as a poet. Oh, how I'll use all womankind hereafter! What would I give to have one of 'em within my reach now! Any mortal thing in petticoats, kind fortune, lend me, and I'll forgive thy last night's malice. Here's a cursed book too (a warning to all young travellers) that can instruct me how to prevent such mischiefs now 'tis too late; well, 'tis a rare convenient thing to read a little now and then, as well as hawk and hunt.

Sits down again and reads.

Enter to him Florinda.

FLORINDA.

This house is haunted sure; 'tis well furnished and no living thing inhabits it — hah — a man; heavens, how he's attired! Sure 'tis

5

10

15

20

---

7 morris dancer] participant in a traditional English dance performed by men in loose
  light clothing, wearing bells and sometimes carrying swords

some rope-dancer, or fencing-master; I tremble now for fear, and yet I must venture now to speak to him. Sir, if I may not interrupt your meditations —

He† starts up and gazes.

BLUNT.

Hah — what's here! Are my wishes granted? And is not that a she creature? 'Sheartlikins, 'tis! What wretched thing art thou — hah!

FLORINDA.

Charitable sir, you've told yourself already what I am, a very wretched maid, forced by a strange unlucky accident to seek safety here, And must be ruined, if you do not grant it.

BLUNT.

Ruined! Is there any ruin so inevitable as that which now threatens thee? Dost thou know, miserable woman, into what den of mischiefs thou art fallen? What abyss of confusion — hah! Dost not see something in my looks that frights thy guilty soul, and makes thee wish to change that shape of woman for any humble animal or devil? For those were safer for thee, and less mischievous.

FLORINDA.

Alas, what mean you, sir? I must confess, your looks have something in 'em makes me fear, but I beseech you, as you seem a gentleman, pity a harmless virgin that takes your house for sanctuary.

BLUNT.

Talk on, talk on, and weep too, till my faith return. Do, flatter me out of my senses again — a harmless virgin with a pox, as much one as t'other, 'sheartlikins. Why, what the devil, can I not be safe in my house for you, not in my chamber, nay, even being naked too cannot secure me; this is an impudence greater than has invaded me yet — come, no resistance.

Pulls her rudely.

---

21 rope-dancer] A performer who danced or did acrobatics on a tight rope or slack rope; like a morris dancer or fencing master, a rope-dancer would wear loose, light clothing.

FLORINDA.

Dare you be so cruel?

BLUNT.

Cruel? 'Sheartlikins, as a galley slave, or a Spanish whore. Cruel?
Yes; I will kiss and beat thee all over, kiss and see thee all over;
thou shalt lie with me too, not that I care for the enjoyment, but   50
to let thee see I have ta'en[†] deliberated malice to thee, and will
be revenged on one whore for the sins of another. I will smile
and deceive thee, flatter thee, and beat thee, kiss and swear and
lie to thee, embrace thee and rob thee, as she did me; fawn on
thee and strip thee stark naked; then hang thee out at my win-   55
dow by the heels, with a paper of scurvy verses fastened to thy
breast, in praise of damnable women — come, come along.

FLORINDA.

Alas, sir, must I be sacrificed for the crimes of the most infamous
of my sex? I never understood the sins you name.

BLUNT.

Do, persuade the fool you love him, or that one of you can be   60
just or honest; tell me I was not an easy coxcomb, or any strange
impossible tale. It will be believed sooner than by false showers
or protestations. A generation of damned hypocrites to flatter
my very clothes from my back! Dissembling witches! Are these
the returns you make an honest gentleman, that trusts, believes,   65
and loves you — but if I be not even with you — come along — or I
shall —

Pulls her again.

Enter Frederick.

FREDERICK.

Hah! What's here to do?

BLUNT.

'Sheartlikins, Frederick. I am glad thou art come to be a witness
of my dire revenge.   70

FREDERICK.

What's this, a person of quality too, who is upon the ramble to
supply the defects of some grave impotent husband?

BLUNT.

No, this has another pretence; some very unfortunate accident
brought her hither, to save a life pursued by I know not who, or

why, and forced to take sanctuary here at Fool's Haven. 'Sheart-likins, to me of all mankind for protection? Is the ass to be ca-joled again, think ye? No, young one, no prayers or tears shall mitigate my rage; therefore prepare for both my pleasures of en-joyment and revenge, for I am resolved to make up my loss here on thy body; I'll take it out in kindness and in beating.

FREDERICK.

Now, mistress of mine, what do you think of this?

FLORINDA.

I think he will not — dares not — be so barbarous.

FREDERICK.

Have a care, Blunt, she fetched a deep sigh; she is enamoured with thy shirt and drawers. She'll strip thee even of that, there are of her calling such unconscionable baggages, and such dextrous thieves, they'll flay[†] a man and he shall ne'er miss his skin till he feels the cold. There was a countryman of ours robbed of a row of teeth whilst he was a-sleeping, which the jilt made him buy again when he waked — you see, lady, how little reason we have to trust you.

BLUNT.

'Sheartlikins, why this is most abominable.

FLORINDA.

Some such devils there may be, but by all that's holy, I am none such; I entered here to save a life in danger.

BLUNT.

For no goodness, I'll warrant her.

FREDERICK.

Faith, damsel, you had e'en confessed the plain truth, for we are fellows not to be caught twice in the same trap. Look on that wreck, a tight vessel when he set out of haven, well trimmed and laden, and see how a female picaroon of this island of rogues has shattered him, and canst thou hope for any mercy?

BLUNT.

No, no, gentlewoman, come along; 'sheartlikins, we must be bet-ter acquainted — we'll both lie with her, and then let me alone to bang her.

FREDERICK.

I'm ready to serve you in matters of revenge that has a double pleasure in't.

BLUNT.

Well said. You hear, little one, how you are condemned by public   105
vote to the bed within; there's no resisting your destiny, sweetheart.

Pulls her.

FLORINDA.

Stay, sir; I have seen you with Belvile, an English cavalier; for his
sake use me kindly; you know him, sir.

BLUNT.

Belvile, why yes, sweeting, we do know Belvile, and wish he were   110
with us now; he's a cormorant at whore and bacon; he'd have a
limb or two of thee, my virgin pullet, but 'tis no matter, we'll
leave him the bones to pick.

FLORINDA.

Sir, if you have any esteem for that Belvile, I conjure you to treat
me with more gentleness; he'll thank you for the justice.   115

FREDERICK.

Harkee, Blunt, I doubt we are mistaken in this matter.

FLORINDA.

Sir, if you find me not worth Belvile's care, use me as you please,
and that you may think I merit better treatment than you
threaten — pray take this present —

Gives him a ring; he looks on it.

BLUNT.

Hum — a diamond! Why 'tis a wonderful virtue now that lies in   120
this ring, a mollifying virtue; 'sheartlikins, there's more persua-
sive rhetoric in't than all her sex can utter.

FREDERICK.

I begin to suspect something; and 'twould anger us vilely to be
trussed up for a rape upon a maid of quality, when we only believe we ruffle a harlot.   125

---

111 cormorant] marine bird known for its voracious appetite

BLUNT.

Thou art a credulous fellow, but 'sheartlikins I have no faith yet;
why my saint prattled as parlously as this does, she gave me a
bracelet too, a devil on her, but I sent my man to sell it today for
necessaries, and it proved as counterfeit as her vows of love.

FREDERICK.

However, let it reprieve her till we see Belvile.

BLUNT.

That's hard, yet I will grant it.

Enter a servant.

SERVANT.

Oh, sir, the colonel is just come in with his new friend and a
Spaniard of quality, and talks of having you to dinner with 'em.

BLUNT.

'Sheartlikins, I'm undone — I would not see 'em for the world.
Harkee, Frederick, lock up the wench in your chamber.

FREDERICK.

Fear nothing, madam; whate'er he threatens, you are safe whilst
in my hands.

Exeunt Frederick and Florinda.

BLUNT.

And, sirrah, upon your life, say — I am not at home — or that I'm
asleep — or — or anything — away — I'll prevent their coming this
way.

ACT V.

Scene I. Blunt's Chamber.

*After a great knocking as at his chamber door, enter Blunt softly crossing the
stage, in his shirt and drawers as before.*

Call within.

VOICES.[†]

Ned, Ned Blunt, Ned Blunt.

BLUNT.

The rogues are up in arms. 'Sheartlikins, this villainous Frederick
has betrayed me; they have heard of my blessed fortune.

Knocking within.

VOICES.[†]

Ned Blunt, Ned, Ned —

BELVILE. [*Within.*][‡]

Why he's dead, sir, without dispute dead, he has not been seen   5
today; let's break open the door — here — boy —

BLUNT.

Ha, break open the door. 'Sheartlikins, that mad fellow will be as
good as his word.

BELVILE. [*Within.*][‡]

Boy, bring something to force the door.

A great noise within, at the door again.

BLUNT.

So, now must I speak in my own defence; I'll try what rhetoric   10
will do — hold — hold; what do you mean gentlemen, what do
you mean?

BELVILE. [*Within.*][‡]

Oh rogue, art alive; prithee open the door and convince us.

BLUNT.

Yes, I am alive gentlemen — but at present a little busy.

BELVILE. [*Within.*][‡]

How, Blunt grown man of business? Come, come, open and let's   15
see this miracle.

BLUNT.

No, no, no, no, gentlemen, 'tis no great business — but — I am —
at — my devotion — 'sheartlikins, will you not allow a man time to
pray?

BELVILE.   [*Within.*]‡

Turned religious! A greater wonder than the first, therefore open   2
quickly, or we shall unhinge, we shall.

BLUNT.

This won't do — why harkee, colonel, to tell you the plain truth, I
am about a necessary affair of life — I have a wench with me —
you apprehend me? The devil's in't if they be so uncivil as to disturb me now.   2

WILLMORE.   [*Within.*]‡

How, a wench! Nay then, we must enter and partake no resistance — unless it be your lady of quality, and then we'll keep our
distance.

BLUNT.

So, the business is out.

WILLMORE.   [*Within.*]‡

Come, come, lend's more hands to the door — now heave alto-   3
gether — so, well done, my boys —

Breaks open the door.

Enter Belvile, Willmore, Frederick, Pedro and Boy.† *Blunt looks simply, they
all laugh at him, he lays his hand on his sword, and comes up to Willmore.*

BLUNT.

Harkee sir, laugh out your laugh quickly, d'ye hear, and begone.
I shall spoil your sport else, 'sheartlikins sir, I shall — the jest has
been carried on too long. [*Aside.*] Oh — a plague upon my tailor.

WILLMORE.

'Sdeath, how the whore has dressed him. Faith, sir, I'm sorry.   3

BLUNT.

Are you so, sir; keep't to yourself then, sir, I advise you, d'ye
hear, for I can as little endure your pity as his mirth.

Lays his hand on's sword.

BELVILE.

Indeed, Willmore, thou wert a little too rough with Ned Blunt's
mistress. Call a person of quality whore? And one so young, so
handsome, and so eloquent — ha, ha, he.   4

BLUNT.

Harkee sir, you know me, and know I can be angry; have a care —
for, 'sheartlikins, I can fight too — I can, sir — do you mark me —
no more —

BELVILE.

Why so peevish, good Ned; some disappointments I'll warrant —
what? Did the jealous count her husband return just in the nick?   45

BLUNT.

Or the devil sir — d'ye laugh —

They laugh.

Look ye settle me a good sober countenance, and that quickly
too, or you shall know Ned Blunt is not —

BELVILE.

Not everybody, we know that.

BLUNT.

Not an ass to be laughed at, sir.   50

WILLMORE.

Unconscionable sinner, to bring a lover so near his happiness, a
vigorous, passionate lover, and then not only cheat him of his
movables, but his very desires too.†

BELVILE.

Ah! Sir, a mistress is a trifle with Blunt. He'll have a dozen the
next time he looks abroad. His eyes have charms not to be re-   55
sisted; there needs no more than† to expose that taking person to
the view of the fair, and he leads 'em all in triumph.

PEDRO.

Sir, though I'm a stranger to you, I am ashamed at the rudeness
of my nation; and could you learn who did it, would assist you to
make an example of 'em.   60

BLUNT.

Why ay, there's one speaks sense now, and han'somely; and let
me tell you, gentlemen, I should not have showed myself like a
Jack Pudding, thus to have made you mirth, but that I have revenge within my power. For know, I have got into my possession
a female who had better have fallen under any curse than the   65

---

63 Jack Pudding] a clown or buffoon; clowning assistant to a mountebank or street
performer; a merry Andrew.

ruin I design her; 'sheartlikins, she assaulted me here in my own lodgings, and had doubtless committed a rape upon me, had not this sword defended me.

FREDERICK.

I know not that, but o'my[†] conscience, thou had ravished her, had she not redeemed herself with a ring — let's see't, Blunt.   70

Blunt shows the ring.

BELVILE.

[*Aside*] The ring I gave Florinda, when we exchanged[†] our vows — harkee Blunt —

Goes to whisper to him.

WILLMORE.

No whispering, good colonel, there's a woman in the case; no whispering.

BELVILE.

Harkee fool, be advised, and conceal both the ring and the story   75
for your reputation's sake. Do not let people know what despised cullies we English are, to be cheated and abused by one whore, and another rather bribe thee than be kind to thee is an infamy to our nation.

WILLMORE.

Come, come, where's the wench? We'll see her, let her be what   80
she will; we'll see her.

PEDRO.

Ay, ay, let us see her. I can soon discover whether she be of quality, or for your diversion.

BLUNT.

She's in Fred's custody.

WILLMORE.

Come, come, the key.   85

To Frederick who gives him the key; they are going.

BELVILE.

Death, what shall I do — Stay gentlemen — yet if I hinder 'em, I shall discover all — hold — let's go at once — give me the key.

WILLMORE.

Nay, hold there colonel; I'll go first.

FREDERICK.   90

Nay, no dispute; Ned and I have the propriety of her.

WILLMORE.

Damn propriety — then we'll draw cuts — [*Belvile goes to whisper to Willmore.*] nay, no corruption, good colonel. Come, the longest sword carries her —

They all draw, forgetting Don Pedro, being as a Spaniard, had the longest.

BLUNT.

I yield up my interest to you, gentlemen, and that will be revenge sufficient.

WILLMORE. [*To Pedro.*]

The wench is yours —   95

[*Aside.*] Pox of his Toledo; I had forgot that.

FREDERICK.

Come sir, I'll conduct you to the lady.

Exeunt Frederick and Pedro.

BELVILE. [*Aside.*]

To hinder him will certainly discover her —
— Dost know, dull beast, what mischief thou hast done?

Willmore walking up and down out of humour.

WILLMORE.

Ay, ay, to trust our fortune to lots, a devil on't; 'twas madness,   100
that's the truth on't.

BELVILE.

Oh intolerable sot —

Stage Direction: longest] reference to a Spanish fashion for long swords
96 Toledo] sword made in Toledo, famous for its fine steel

Enter Florinda running masked, Pedro after her;
Willmore gazing round her.

FLORINDA. [*Aside.*]
Good heaven, defend me from discovery.
PEDRO.
'Tis but in vain to fly me, you're fallen to my lot.
BELVILE.
Sure she's undiscovered yet, but now I fear there is no way to   1●
bring her off.
WILLMORE.
Why, what a pox; is not this my woman, the same I followed but
now?

Pedro talking to Florinda, who walks up and down.

PEDRO.
As if I did not know ye, and your business here.
FLORINDA. [*Aside.*]
Good heaven, I fear he does indeed —   1●
PEDRO.
Come, pray be kind; I know you meant to be so when you en-
tered here, for these are proper gentlemen.
WILLMORE.
But sir — perhaps the lady will not be imposed upon. She'll
choose her man.
PEDRO.
I am better bred, than† not to leave her choice free.   1●

Enter Valeria, and is surprised at sight of Don Pedro.

VALERIA. [*Aside.*]
Don Pedro here! There's no avoiding him.
FLORINDA. [*Aside.*]
Valeria! Then I'm undone —
VALERIA.
Oh! Have I found you, sir —

To Pedro, running to him.

— the strangest accident — if I had breath — to tell it.

PEDRO.

    Speak — is Florinda safe? Hellena well? 120

VALERIA.

    Ay, ay sir — Florinda — is safe — from any fears of you.

PEDRO.

    Why, where's Florinda? Speak —

VALERIA.

    Ay, where indeed sir, I wish I could inform you — but to hold you
no longer in doubt —

FLORINDA.   [*Aside.*]

    Oh, what will she say —' 125

VALERIA.

    She's fled away in the habit — of one of her pages, sir — but Callis
thinks you may retrieve her yet. If you make haste away, she'll tell
you, sir, the rest — [*Aside.*] if you can find her out.

PEDRO.

    Dishonourable girl, she has undone my aim. Sir — you see my ne-
cessity of leaving you, and hope you'll pardon it; my sister, I 130
know, will make her flight to you; and if she do, I shall expect she
should be rendered back.

BELVILE.

    I shall consult my love and honour, sir.

Exit Pedro.

FLORINDA.   [*To Valeria.*]

    My dear preserver, let me embrace thee.

WILLMORE.

    What the devil's all this? 135

BLUNT.

    Mystery by this light.

VALERIA.

    Come, come, make haste and get yourselves married quickly, for
your brother will return again.

BELVILE.

    I'm so surprised with fears and joys, so amazed to find you here in
safety, I can scarce persuade my heart into a faith of what I see. 140

WILLMORE.

    Harkee colonel, is this that mistress who has cost you so many
sighs, and me so many quarrels with you?

BELVILE.

It is — [*To Florinda*] Pray give him the honour of your hand.

WILLMORE.

Thus it must be received then.

Kneels and kisses her hand.

And with it give your pardon, too.   145

FLORINDA.

The friend to Belvile may command me anything.

WILLMORE.   [*Aside.*]

Death, would I might; 'tis a surprising beauty.

BELVILE.

Boy, run and fetch a father instantly.

Exit Boy.

FREDERICK.

So, now do I stand like a dog, and have not a syllable to plead my
own cause with; by this hand, madam, I was never thoroughly   150
confounded before, nor shall I ever more dare look up with con-
fidence, till you are pleased to pardon me.

FLORINDA.

Sir, I'll be reconciled to you on one condition, that you'll follow
the example of your friend, in marrying a maid that does not
hate you, and whose fortune (I believe) will not be unwelcome to   155
you.

FREDERICK.

Madam, had I no inclinations that way, I should obey your kind
commands.

BELVILE.

Who, Frederick marry? He has so few inclinations for womankind, that had he been possessed of paradise he might have con-   160
tinued there to this day, if no crime but love could have disinher-
ited him.

FREDERICK.

Oh, I do not use to boast of my intrigues.

BELVILE.

Boast, why thou dost nothing but boast; and I dare swear, wert
thou as innocent from the sin of the grape, as thou art from the   165

apple, thou might'st yet claim that right in Eden which our first
parents lost by too much loving.

FREDERICK.

. I wish this lady would think me so modest a man.

VALERIA.

She would be sorry then, and not like you half as well, and I
should be loath to break my word with you, which was, that if   170
your friend and mine agreed, it should be a match between you
and I.

She gives him her hand.

FREDERICK.

Bear witness, colonel, 'tis a bargain.

Kisses her hand.

BLUNT.   [*To Florinda.*]

I have a pardon to beg too, but 'sheartlikins, I am so out of countenance that I'm a dog if I can say anything to purpose.   175

FLORINDA.

Sir, I heartily forgive you all.

BLUNT.

That's nobly said, sweet lady — Belvile, prithee present her her
ring again; for I find I have not courage to approach her myself.

Gives him the ring; he gives it[†] *to Florinda.*

Enter Boy.

BOY.

Sir, I have brought the father that you sent for.

BELVILE.

'Tis well, and now my dear Florinda, let's fly to complete that   180
mighty joy we have so long wished and sighed for. Come
Frederick — you'll follow?

FREDERICK.

Your example, sir, 'twas ever my ambition in war, and must be so
in love.

WILLMORE.

And must not I see this juggling knot tied?   185

BELVILE.

No, thou shalt do us better service, and be our guard, lest Don Pedro's sudden return interrupt the ceremony.

WILLMORE.

Content — I'll secure this pass.

Exeunt Belvile, Florinda, Frederick and Valeria.

Enter Boy.

BOY. [*To Willmore.*]

Sir, there's a lady without would speak to you.

WILLMORE.

Conduct her in, I dare not quit my post.   190

BOY.

And sir, your tailor waits you in your chamber.

BLUNT.

Some comfort yet, I shall not dance naked at the wedding.

Exeunt Blunt and Boy.

Enter again the Boy, conducting in
Angellica in a masquing habit and a vizard. Willmore runs to her.

WILLMORE.

This can be none but my pretty gypsy — oh, I see you can follow as well as fly. Come, confess thyself the most malicious devil in nature; you think you have done my business with Angellica —   195

ANGELLICA.

Stand off, base villain —

She draws a pistol, and holds it to his breast.

WILLMORE.

Hah, 'tis not she; who art thou? And what's thy business?

ANGELLICA.

One thou hast injured, and who comes to kill thee for't.

WILLMORE.

What the devil canst thou mean?

ANGELLICA.

By all my hopes to kill thee —   200

Holds still the pistol to his breast, he going back, she following still.

WILLMORE.

Prithee, on what acquaintance? For I know thee not.

ANGELLICA.

Behold this face — so lost to thy remembrance,
And then call all thy sins about thy soul,

Pulls off her vizard.

And let 'em die with thee.

WILLMORE.

Angellica!   205

ANGELLICA.

Yes, traitor,†
Does not thy guilty blood run shivering through thy veins?
Hast thou no horror at this sight that tells thee
Thou hast not long to boast thy shameful conquest?

WILLMORE.

Faith, no, child; my blood keeps its old ebbs and flows still, and   210
that usual heat too, that could oblige thee with a kindness, had I
but opportunity.

ANGELLICA.

Devil! Dost wanton with my pain — have at thy heart.

WILLMORE.

Hold, dear virago! Hold thy hand a little; I am not now at leisure
to be killed — hold and hear me —   215
[*Aside*] — Death, I think she's in earnest.

ANGELLICA.   [*Aside, turning from him.*]
Oh, if I take not heed,
My coward heart will leave me to his mercy.
— What have you, sir, to say? But should I hear thee,
Thou'dst talk away all that is brave about me: 220

Follows him with the pistol to his breast.

And I have vowed thy death, by all that's sacred.

---

214 virago] strong or angry woman; a female warrior

WILLMORE.

> Why, then there's an end of a proper handsome fellow,
> That might 'a' lived to have done good service yet;
> That's all I can say to't.

ANGELLICA.   [*Pausingly.*]

> Yet — I would give thee — time for — penitence.   2

WILLMORE.

> Faith child, I thank God I have ever took
> Care to lead a good sober, hopeful life, and am of a religion
> That teaches me to believe I shall depart in peace.

ANGELLICA.

> So will the devil! Tell me,
> How many poor believing fools thou hast undone?   2
> How many hearts thou hast betrayed to ruin?
> Yet these are little mischiefs to the ills
> Thou'st taught mine to commit: thou'st taught it love.

WILLMORE.

> Egad, 'twas shrewdly hurt the while.

ANGELLICA.

> Love, that has robbed it of its unconcern   2
> Of all that pride that taught me how to value it.
> And in its room
> A mean submissive passion was conveyed,
> That made me humbly bow, which I ne'er did
> To any thing but heaven.   24
> Thou, perjured man, didst this, and with thy oaths,
> Which on thy knees, thou didst devoutly make,
> Softened my yielding heart — and then, I was a slave —
> Yet still had been content to've worn my chains,
> Worn 'em with vanity and joy for ever,   24
> Hadst thou not broke those vows that put them on.
> 'Twas then I was undone.

> *All this while follows him with the pistol to his breast.*

WILLMORE.

> Broke my vows! Why, where hast thou lived?
> Amongst the gods? For I never heard of mortal man
> That has not broke a thousand vows.   2

ANGELLICA.

> Oh impudence!

WILLMORE.

    Angellica! That beauty has been too long tempting

    Not to have made a thousand lovers languish,

    Who in the amorous fever† no doubt have sworn

    Like me; did they all die in that faith? Still adoring?   255

    I do not think they did.

ANGELLICA.

    No, faithless man; had I repaid their vows, as I did thine,

    I would have killed the ingrateful that had abandoned me.

WILLMORE.

    This old general has quite spoiled thee; nothing makes a woman

    so vain as being flattered. Your old lover ever supplies the de-   260

    fects of age, with intolerable dotage, vast charge, and that which

    you call constancy; and attributing this to your own merits, you

    domineer, and throw your favours in's teeth, upbraiding him still

    with the defects of age, and cuckold him as often as he deceives

    your expectations. But the gay, young, brisk lover that brings his   265

    equal fires, and can give you dart for dart, will be† as nice as you

    sometimes.

ANGELLICA.

    All this thou'st made me know, for which I hate thee.

    Had I remained in innocent security,

    I should have thought all men were born my slaves,   270

    And worn my pow'r like lightning in my eyes,

    To have destroyed at pleasure when offended.

    But when love held the mirror, the undeceiving glass

    Reflected all the weakness of my soul, and made me know

    My richest treasure being lost, my honour,   275

    All the remaining spoil could not be worth

    The conqueror's care or value.

    Oh how I fell, like a long worshipped idol

    Discovering all the cheat.

    Would not the incense and rich sacrifice   280

    Which blind devotion offered at my altars,

    Have fall'n to thee?

    Why wouldst thou then destroy my fancied pow'r?

WILLMORE.

    By heaven thou'rt brave, and I admire thee strangely.

    I wish I were that dull, that constant thing   285

    Which thou wouldst have, and nature never meant me.

    I must, like cheerful birds, sing in all groves,

And perch on every bough,
Billing the next kind she that flies to meet me;
Yet after all could build my nest with thee,   290
Thither repairing when I'd loved my round,
And still reserve a tributary flame.
To gain your credit, I'll pay you back your charity,
And be obliged for nothing but for love.

Offers her a purse of gold.

ANGELLICA.
Oh that thou wert in earnest!   295
So mean a thought of me,
Would turn my rage to scorn, and I should pity thee,
And give thee leave to live;
Which for the public safety of our sex,
And my own private injuries, I dare not do,   300
Prepare —

Follows still, as before.

I will no more be tempted with replies.
WILLMORE.
Sure —
ANGELLICA.
Another word will damn thee! I've heard thee talk too long.

She follows him with the pistol ready to shoot; he retires still amazed.

Enter Don Antonio, his arm in a scarf, and lays hold on the pistol.†

ANTONIO.
Hah! Angellica!   305
ANGELLICA.
Antonio! What devil brought thee hither?
ANTONIO.
Love and curiosity, seeing your coach at door.
Let me disarm you of this unbecoming instrument of death —

Takes away the pistol.

Amongst the number of your slaves, was there not one worthy
the honour to have fought your quarrel?   310
 — Who are you sir, that are so very wretched
To merit death from her?

WILLMORE.

One, sir, that could have made a better end of an amorous quarrel without you, than with you.

ANTONIO.

Sure 'tis some rival — hah — the very man took down her picture   315
yesterday — the very same that set on me last night — blest opportunity —

Offers to shoot him.

ANGELLICA.

Hold, you're mistaken sir.

ANTONIO.

By heaven, the very same!
Sir, what pretensions have you to this lady?   320

WILLMORE.

Sir, I do not use to be examined, and am ill at all disputes but
this —

Draws; Antonio offers to shoot.

ANGELLICA.   [*To Willmore.*]

Oh hold! You see he's armed with certain death,
 — And you Antonio, I command you hold,
By all the passion you've so lately vowed me.   325

Enter Don Pedro, sees Antonio and stays.

PEDRO.   [*Aside.*]

Hah, Antonio! And Angellica!

ANTONIO.

When I refuse obedience to your will,
May you destroy me with your mortal hate.
By all that's holy I adore you so,
That even my rival, who has charms enough   330
To make him fall a victim to my jealousy
Shall live, nay and have leave to love on still.

PEDRO. [*Aside.*]
   What's this I hear?
ANGELLICA.
   Ah thus! 'Twas thus he talked, and I believed.

   Pointing to Willmore.

   Antonio,[†] yesterday,   33
   I'd not have sold my interest in his heart
   For all the sword has won and lost in battle.
   But now to show my utmost of contempt,
   I give thee life — which if thou wouldst preserve,
   Live where my eyes may never see thee more,   34
   Live to undo someone whose soul may prove
   So bravely constant to revenge my love.

      Goes out, Antonio follows, but Pedro pulls him back.

PEDRO.
   Antonio — stay.
ANTONIO.
   Don Pedro —
PEDRO.
   What coward fear was that prevented thee   34
   From meeting me this morning on the Molo?
ANTONIO.
   Meet thee?
PEDRO.
   Yes me; I was the man that dared thee to't.
ANTONIO.
   Hast thou so often seen me fight in war,
   To find no better cause to excuse my absence?   35
   I sent my sword and one to do thee right,
   Finding myself uncapable to use a sword.
PEDRO.
   But 'twas Florinda's quarrel we fought,
   And you, to show how little you esteemed her,
   Sent me your rival, giving him your interest.
   But I have found the cause of this affront,   35
   And when I meet you fit for the dispute,
   I'll tell you my resentment.

ANTONIO.

    I shall be ready, sir, ere long, to do you reason.

Exit Antonio.

PEDRO.

    If I could find Florinda now whilst my anger's high, I think I 360
should be kind, and give her to Belvile in revenge.

WILLMORE.

    Faith, sir, I know not what you would do, but I believe the priest
within has been so kind.

PEDRO.

    How! My sister married?

WILLMORE.

    I hope by this time he† is, and bedded too, or he has not my 365
longings about him.

PEDRO.

    Dares he do this! Does he not fear my power?

WILLMORE.

    Faith, not at all. If you will go in, and thank him for the favour he
has done your sister, so; if not, sir, my power's greater in this
house than yours. I have a damned surly crew here, that will keep 370
you till the next tide, and then clap you on board for prize;† my
ship lies but a league off the Molo, and we shall show your don-
ship a damned tramontana rover's trick.

Enter Belvile.

BELVILE.

    This rogue's in some new mischief — hah, Pedro returned!

PEDRO.

    Colonel Belvile, I hear you have married my sister? 375

BELVILE.

    You have heard the truth then, sir.

PEDRO.

    Have I so; then, sir, I wish you joy.

---

373 tramontana] lit., a person from the other side of the mountains; fig., a foreigner,
barbarian

BELVILE.

How!

PEDRO.

By this embrace I do, and I am glad on't.

BELVILE.

Are you in earnest?   3

PEDRO.

By our long friendship and my obligations to thee, I am,
The sudden change I'll give you reasons for anon.
Come lead me to my sister,
That she may know I now approve her choice.

*Exeunt Belvile with Pedro. Willmore goes to follow them. Enter Hellena as
before in boy's clothes, and pulls him back.*

WILLMORE.

Ha! My gypsy — now a thousand blessings on thee for this kind-   38
ness. Egad child, I was e'en in despair of ever seeing thee again;
my friends are all provided for within, each man his kind woman.

HELLENA.

Ha! I thought they had served me some such trick!

WILLMORE.

And I was e'en resolved to go aboard, and condemn myself to
my lone cabin, and the thoughts of thee.   39

HELLENA.

And could you have left me behind, would you have been so ill
natured?

WILLMORE.

Why, 'twould have broke my heart, child — but since we are met
again, I defy foul weather to part us.

HELLENA.

And would you be a faithful friend now, if a maid should trust   39
you?

WILLMORE.

For a friend I cannot promise; thou art of a form so excellent, a
face and humour too good for cold dull friendship. I am parlously afraid of being in love, child, and you have not forgot how
severely you have used me?   40

HELLENA.

That's all one; such usage you must still look for, to find out all
your haunts, to rail at you to all that love you, till I have made

you love only me in your own defence, because nobody else will love you.[†]

WILLMORE.

But hast thou no better quality to recommend thyself by?   405

HELLENA.

Faith, none, captain — why, 'twill be the greater charity to take me for thy mistress. I am alone, child, a kind of orphan lover, and why I should die a maid, and in a captain's hands too, I do not understand.

WILLMORE.

Egad, I was never clawed away with broadsides from any female   410 before. Thou hast one virtue I adore, good nature. I hate a coy demure mistress, she's as troublesome as a colt; I'll break none. No, give me a mad mistress when mewed, and in flying, one[†] I dare trust upon the wing, that whilst she's kind will come to the lure.   415

HELLENA.

Nay, as kind as you will, good captain, whilst it lasts, but let's lose no time.

WILLMORE.

My time's as precious to me as thine can be; therefore dear creature, since we are so well agreed, let's retire to my chamber, and if ever thou wert treated with such savoury love! Come — my   420 bed's prepared for such a guest, all clean and sweet as thy fair self. I love to steal a dish and a bottle with a friend, and hate long graces — come let's retire and fall to.[†]

HELLENA.

'Tis but getting my consent, and the business is soon done. Let but old gaffer Hymen and his priest say amen to't, and I dare lay   425 my mother's daughter by as proper a fellow as your father's son, without fear or blushing.

---

410 broadside] a single sheet of paper printed on one side. Ballads were customarily published on broadsides; Hellena's references to an orphan lover and a captain are characteristic of ballad themes.

413 mewed] of hawks, confined in a cage. Willmore's speech makes several references to hawking, in which a hawk is sent to hunt other birds, and encouraged to return by a lure.

425 gaffer] old man

425 Hymen] god of marriage

WILLMORE.

> Hold, hold, no bug words, child; priest and Hymen? Prithee add a hangman to 'em to make up the consort — no, no, we'll have no vows but love, child, nor witness but the lover; the kind deity enjoins[†] naught but love and enjoy! Hymen and priest wait still upon portion, and jointure; love and beauty have their own ceremonies. Marriage is as certain a bane to love as lending money is to friendship. I'll neither ask nor give a vow — though I could be content to turn gypsy, and become a left-handed bridegroom to have the pleasure of working that great miracle of making a maid a mother, if you durst venture; 'tis upse gypsy that, and if I miss, I'll lose my labour.

HELLENA.

> And if you do not lose, what shall I get? A cradle full of noise and mischief, with a pack of repentance at my back? Can you teach me to weave incle to pass my time with? 'Tis upse gypsy that too.

WILLMORE.

> I can teach thee to weave a true love's knot better.

HELLENA.

> So can my dog.

WILLMORE.

> Well, I see we are both upon our guards, and I see there's no way to conquer good nature, but by yielding — here — give me thy hand — one kiss and I am thine —

HELLENA.

> One kiss! How like my page he speaks; I am resolved you shall have none, for asking such a sneaking sum. He that will be satisfied with one kiss, will never die of that longing. Good friend single kiss, is all your talking come to this? A kiss, a caudle! Farewell captain single kiss.

430

435

440

445

450

---

428 bug words] frightening words; related to "bogey"
432 portion and jointure] financial arrangements made as part of a marriage agreement; portion — money a woman brings to her husband in marriage; jointure — provision for support of a wife after husband's death
435 left-handed bridegroom] without a legal marriage
437 upse] in the manner or fashion of
441 incle] linen thread, used to weave tape
442 true love's knot] an elaborate knot symbolizing love.
450 caudle] gruel for invalid

Going out; he stays her.

WILLMORE.

Nay, if we part so, let me die like a bird upon a bough, at the
sheriff's charge. By heaven, both the Indies shall not buy thee
from me. I adore thy humour and will marry thee, and we are so
of one humour, it must be a bargain — give me thy hand —   455

Kisses her hand.

And now let the blind ones (love and fortune) do their worst.

HELLENA.

Why, god-a-mercy, captain!

WILLMORE.

But harkee — the bargain is now made; but is it not fit we should
know each other's names, that when we have reason to curse one
another hereafter (and people ask me who 'tis I give to the devil)   460
I may at least be able to tell what family you came of.

HELLENA.

Good reason, captain; and where I have cause (as I doubt not but
I shall have plentiful) that I may know at whom to throw my —
blessings — I beseech ye your name.

WILLMORE.

I am called Robert the Constant.   465

HELLENA.

A very fine name; pray was it your falconer or butler that chris-
tened you? Do they not use to whistle when they call you?

WILLMORE.

I hope you have a better, that a man may name without crossing
himself; you are merry with mine.

HELLENA.

I am called Hellena the Inconstant.   470

Enter Pedro, Belvile, Florinda, Frederick, Valeria.

---

456 blind ones, (love and fortune)] In art, both Cupid, god of love, and Lady Fortune are
  depicted blindfolded.
466 falconer] keeper of hawks

PEDRO.

Hah! Hellena!

FLORINDA.

Hellena!

HELLENA.

The very same — hah, my brother! Now captain, show your love
and courage; stand to your arms, and defend me bravely, or I am
lost for ever.

PEDRO.

What's this I hear! False girl, how came you hither and what's
your business? Speak.

Goes roughly to her.

WILLMORE.

Hold off sir, you have leave to parley only.

Puts himself between.

HELLENA.

I had e'en as good tell it, as you guess it; faith, brother, my business is the same with all living creatures of my age, to love, and
be beloved, and here's the man.

PEDRO.

Perfidious maid, hast thou deceived me too? Deceived thy self
and heaven?

HELLENA.

'Tis time enough to make my peace with that. Be you but kind;
let me alone with heaven.

PEDRO.

Belvile, I did not expect this false play from you; was't not
enough you'd gain Florinda (which I pardoned) but your lewd
friends too must be enriched with the spoils of a noble family?

BELVILE.

Faith sir, I am as much surprised at this as you can be. Yet sir, my
friends are gentlemen, and ought to be esteemed for their mis-

fortunes, since they have the glory to suffer with the best of men
and kings; 'tis true, he's a rover of fortune, yet a prince aboard
his little wooden world.

PEDRO.

What's this to the maintenance of a woman of her birth and quality? 495

WILLMORE.

Faith, sir, I can boast of nothing but a sword which does me right
where'er I come, and has defended a worse cause than a
woman's; and since I loved her before I either knew her birth or
name, I must pursue my resolution, and marry her.

PEDRO.

And is all your holy intent of becoming a nun debauched into a 500
desire of man?

HELLENA.

Why — I have considered the matter, brother, and find the three
hundred thousand crowns my uncle left me (and you cannot
keep from me) will be better laid out in love than in religion, and
turn to as good an account. Let most voices carry it, for heaven 505
or the captain?

ALL CRY.

A captain! A captain!

HELLENA.

Look ye sir, 'tis a clear case.

PEDRO. [*Aside.*]

Oh I am mad — if I refuse, my life's in danger —
— Come — there's one motive induces me — take her — I shall 510
now be free from fears of her honour; guard it you now, if you
can; I have been a slave to't long enough.

Gives her to him.

---

491 the best of men and kings] the future Charles II
503 three hundred thousand crowns] There is some inconsistency about the size of
 Hellena's dowry. Earlier, Angellica tells Willmore that Hellena has two hundred
 thousand crowns.

WILLMORE.

Faith sir, I am of a nation that are of opinion a woman's honour is not worth guarding when she has a mind to part with it.

HELLENA.

Well said, captain.   51

PEDRO.   [*To Valeria.*]

This was your plot, mistress, but I hope you have married one that will revenge my quarrel to you —

VALERIA.

There's no altering destiny, sir.

PEDRO.

Sooner than a woman's will; therefore I forgive you all — and wish you may get my father's pardon as easily, which I fear.   52

*Enter Blunt dressed in a Spanish habit, looking very ridiculously;
his man adjusting his band.*

MAN.

'Tis very well, sir —

BLUNT.

Well sir, 'sheartlikins, I tell you 'tis damnable ill, sir — a Spanish habit, good lord! Could the devil and my tailor devise no other punishment for me, but the mode of a nation I abominate?

BELVILE.

What's the matter, Ned?   52:

BLUNT.

Pray view me round, and judge —

Turns round.

BELVILE.

I must confess thou art a kind of an odd figure.

BLUNT.

In a Spanish habit with a vengeance! I had rather be in the inquisition for Judaism, than in this doublet and breeches; a pillory were an easy collar to this, three handfuls high; and these shoes   53(
too, are worse than the stocks, with the sole an inch shorter than

---

Stage Direction: band] neckband

my foot. In fine, gentlemen, methinks I look altogether like a bag of bays stuffed full of fool's flesh.

BELVILE.

Methinks 'tis well, and makes thee look e'n cavalier; come, sir, settle your face, and salute our friends. Lady —   535

BLUNT.

Ha! Say'st thou so my little rover —

To Hellena.

Lady — (if you be one), give me leave to kiss your hand, and tell you, 'sheartlikins, for all I look so, I am your humble servant — a pox of my Spanish habit.

Music is heard to play. Enter Boy.

WILLMORE.

Hark — what's this?   540

BOY.

Sir, as the custom is, the gay people in masquerade who make every man's house their own are coming up.

Enter several men and women in masquing habits with music; they put themselves in order and dance.

BLUNT.   [*Of the masquers.*]†

'Sheartlikins, would 'twere lawful to pull off their false faces, that I might see if my doxy were not among'st 'em.

BELVILE.

Ladies and gentlemen, since you are come so *a propos*, you must   545
take a small collation with us.

WILLMORE.

Whilst we'll to the good man within, who stays to give us a cast of his office.

To Hellena.

---

533 bag of bays] (?) a bag of bay leaves used in cooking (Link); Kemble amends to "bag of baize," a thick green cloth.

— Have you no trembling at the near approach?

HELLENA.

No more than you have in an engagement or a tempest.

WILLMORE.

Egad thou'rt a brave girl, and I admire thy love and courage.
Lead on, no other dangers they can dread,
Who venture in the storms o'th' marriage bed.

Exeunt.

THE END.

EPILOGUE

The banished cavaliers! A roving blade!
A Popish carnival! A masquerade!
The devil's in't if this will please the nation,
In these our blessed times of reformation,   5
When conventicling is so much in fashion.
And yet —
That mutinous tribe less factions do beget,
Than your continual differing in wit;
Your judgement's (as your passion's) a disease: 10
Nor muse nor miss your appetite can please;
You're grown as nice as queasy consciences,
Whose each convulsion, when the spirit moves,
Damns every thing that maggot disapproves.
With canting rule you would the stage refine,   15
And to dull method all our sense confine.
With th' insolence of commonwealths you rule,
Where each gay fop, and politic grave fool
On monarch wit impose, without control.
As for the last, who seldom sees a play,   20
Unless it be the old Blackfriars way,
Shaking his empty noddle o'er bamboo,
He cries, "Good faith, these plays will never do.
Ah, sir, in my young days, what lofty wit,
What high strained scenes of fighting there were writ: 25
These are slight airy toys. But tell me, pray,
What has the House of Commons done today?"
Then shows his politics, to let you see,
Of state affairs he'll judge as notably,
As he can do of wit and poetry.

---

1 blade] swordsman; energetic young man

5 conventicling] participating in a religious conventicle, a clandestine meeting of religious
  nonconformists or Dissenters. The "Epilogue" includes a number of references to
  religious groups' disapproval of the theatre on moral grounds.

13 maggot] a whim

20 Blackfriars] a private theatre popular in the early seventeenth century, but closed in
   1642; a style of acting and drama considered old-fashioned in 1677

21 bamboo] a cane

The younger sparks, who hither do resort,
Cry,
"Pox o' your gentle[†] things, give us more sport;
Damn me, I'm sure 'twill never please the court."
Such fops are never pleased unless the play
Be stuffed with fools as brisk and dull as they.
Such might the half-crown spare, and in a glass
At home behold a more accomplished ass,
Where they may set their cravats, wigs and faces,
And practice all their buffoonry grimaces.[†]
See how this huff becomes, this damny, stare —
Which they at home may act, because they dare,
But — must with prudent caution do elsewhere.
Oh that our Nokes, or Tony Lee could show
A fop but half so much to th'life as you.

---

30 sparks] foppish young men
36 half-crown] a coin worth 2s. 6d.
43 Nokes] James Nokes, comic actor (d. 1696)
43 Tony Lee] Anthony Leigh, comic actor (d. 1692)

Post-Script.[†]

This play had been sooner in print, but for a report about the town (made by some either very malicious or very ignorant) that 'twas *Thomaso* altered, which made the booksellers fear some trouble from the proprietor of that admirable play, which indeed has wit enough to stock a poet, and is not to be pieced or   5
mended by any but the excellent author himself. That I have stolen some hints from it, may be a proof that I valued it more than to pretend to alter it, had I had the dexterity of some poets, who are not more expert in stealing than in the art of concealing, and who even that way outdo the Spartan boys. I might have appro-   10
priated all to myself, but I, vainly proud of my judgment, hang out the sign of Angellica (the only stolen object) to give notice where a great part of the wit dwelt; though if the Play of the Novella were as well worth remembering as *Thomaso,* they might (bating the name) have as well said, I took it from thence. I will   15
only say the plot and business (not to boast on't) is my own; as for the words and characters, I leave the reader to judge and compare 'em with *Thomaso,* to whom I recommend the great entertainment of reading it, though had this succeeded ill, I should have had no need of imploring that justice from the critics who   20
are naturally so kind to any that pretend to usurp their dominion, especially of our sex,[†] they would doubtless have give me the whole honour on't. Therefore I will only say in English what the famous Virgil does in Latin; I made verses, and others have the fame.   25

FINIS.

---

3 *Thomaso*] play by Thomas Killigrew. See discussion of sources in "Introduction."
5 pieced] patched
13 Play of the Novella] Richard Brome's *The Novella*. See discussion of sources in "Introduction."

Textual Notes

The copytext is the first edition (Q1). The textual notes indicate the cases in which I have incorporated a reading from an edition other than the first edition. The source of the reading adopted in the text is entered first, followed by sources of variant readings.

The early editions which have been collated for this edition are listed below:

Q1   [Behn, Mrs. A]. *The Rover or, The Banish't Cavaliers*. London: John Amery, 1677. (First edition; quarto). Q1 exists in three issues; only the third issue names Behn (see "A Note on the Text"). I have collated copies from the British Library (BL), Thomas Fisher Rare Books Library, University of Toronto (Fisher), and a microfilm of a copy held by the Huntington Library (Huntington).

Q2   Behn, Mrs. Ann. *The Rover; or, The Banish't Cavaliers*. London: Richard Wellington, MDCXVII [1697]. (Second quarto)

Q3   [Behn, Aphra]. *The Rover, or the Banish'd Cavaliers*. London: Richard Wellington 1709. (Third quarto)

A   *Plays Written by the Late Ingenious Mrs. Behn, Entire in Two Volumes*. London: Tonson and Wellington, MDCCII [1702].

B   Behn, Aphra. *Plays*. 4 vols. London: Mary Poulson, 1724.

I have also consulted the editions by Kemble, Summers and Link listed under "Adaptations and Modern Editions of Behn's Works" in the *Selected Bibliography*.

Speech prefixes and stage directions are found immediately following the line numbers given in the list below.

Prologue

22	correct] Coract Q1
26	gentle] Gentile Q1
42	debauches] Deboches Q1

Actors' Names

1	Jevon] Jevorne Q1.
2	Medbourne] Medburne Q1.
6	Crosby] Crosbie Q1.
7	Blunt] Q2, A, B; Fred. Q1, Q3
11	Percival] Percivall Q1.
17	Diego] *om.* Q1.
19	Boy] *om.* Q1.
21	Barry] Barrer Q1
25	Quin] Gwin Q1. See "Introduction" for a discussion of the confusion between Anne Quin and Nell Gwyn in relation to this role in *The Rover*.
30	Gillow] Gillo Q1.
I.i.45	Pamplona] Pampulona Q1
I.i.64	Colonel] Coll. Q1. All other abbreviations have been silently expanded.
I.i.70	threw] Q3, A,B; through Q1,Q2
I.i.87	a while] awhile Q1
I.i.125	Hotel de Dieu] Hostel de Dieu Q1.
I.i.165	have] Q1,Q3; hate Q2,A,B
I.i.185	Madam] Q3, B; Mad? Q1,Q2,A
I.ii.1	why] The first edition reads "whe", an exclamation used for emphasis or to demand attention; variant of archaic "we" (OED). Since there is no satisfactory modern equivalent for this

now-archaic expression, I have followed the examples of previous editors and changed "whe" to "why" throughout.

I.ii.128   lest] least Q1

I.ii.206   guessed] guest Q1

I.ii.286   geld] gueld Q1

I.ii.313   sale] Sail Q1

II.i.24   BLUNT.] Q3, B; omitted Q1,Q2.

II.i.25   mistress] Mrs. Q1

II.i.26   FREDERICK and speech] runs on from previous line Q1

II.i.27   BLUNT] Q3,A,B; *om.* Q1,Q2.

II.i.33   WILLMORE] Q3; S.P. and speech included in previous line Q1, Q2, A, B.

II.i.34   BLUNT] Q3,A,B; *om.* Q1, Q2.

II.i.81   waist] Waste Q1

II.i.221   a thousand] 1000 Q2,A,B; a 1000 Q1

II.i.226   Hold...fight.] Angellica's line precedes S.D. in Q1,Q2,Q3,A,B.

II.i.267   money] Mo- Q1

II.i.268   FREDERICK] Q3,B; Pedro Q1, Q2, A

II.i.279   Bye] Buy Q1

II.ii.33   pistole] Pistol Q1

II.ii.35   thing] Q3; things Q1,Q2,A,B

II.ii.82   bewitched] Q2, Q3. A, B; bewitch Q1

II.ii.89   though] Q2,Q3,A,B; thou Q1

III.i.7   Loreto] B; Lorreta Q1,Q2,A,B.

III.i.45   would] wou'd Q3; wou't Q1,Q2; won't A,B.

III.i.49   a thousand] Q1 a 1000

III.i.63   not a word] Q2,Q3,A,B; not word Q1.

III.i.78   talk of] Q2, A; talk off Q1, Q3

III.i.83   *Enter Willmore*] Q3; *om.* Q1,Q2,A,B

III.i.84   Ay, ay] I, I Q1

III.i.107   he and she gold] B; he and the gold Q1,Q2; the he and the she gold Q3

III.i.124   lest] least Q1

III.i.143   barest] Q1,Q2,Q3; bearest A,B

III.i.155   'tis] Q3; 'ts Q1; it's Q2; is't A,B

III.i.214   lose] Q2,Q3,A,B; loose Q1

III.i.221   very fair lady] Q1 (BL, Fisher); very lady Q1 (Huntington)

III.i.278   mistress] Q3,B; Mistris Q2,A; Mrs. Q1

III.iii.15   *shirt, drawers, etc.*] Q1 (BL, Fisher),Q3; shirt, drawers Q1 (Huntington), Q2; shirt and drawers A,B

III.iii.29   dispatched] dispatch Q1
III.iii.45   bowed] bowd Q1
III.iii.49   shore] shoar Q1
III.iv.24   *Exit*] Q3; *om.* Q1,Q2,A,B
III.v.58   pistole] Q2,A; pistol Q1, Q3,B
III.v.65   pistole] pistol Q1
III.vi.30   spiteful] Spightful Q1
III.v.63   ANTONIO] Q3,B; *om.* in Q1,Q2,A
IV.ii.13   I] B; *om.* Q1,Q2,Q3,A.
IV.ii.82   lose] Q3,A,B; loose Q1,Q2
IV.ii.114   lose] Q2,Q3,A,B; loose Q1
IV.ii.127   haste] hast Q1
IV.ii.132   aught] ought Q1
IV.ii.211   above] Q1 adove
IV.ii.229   HELLENA] Q2,Q3,A,B; Angellica Q1
IV.ii.260   he] Q3; she Q1,Q2,A,B.
IV.ii.291   devil] divil Q1.
IV.ii.292   in] Q2,Q3,A,B; *om.* Q1.
IV.ii.300   impudentest] Q3; impudent'st Q2,A;B; impudents Q1.
IV.ii.352   WILLMORE] Q3,A,B; *om.* Q1,Q2
IV.iii.17   your letter, your note] Q1(Fisher, Huntington), Q2,Q3,A,B.; your note Q1(BL).
IV.v.23   *He*] Q3,A,B; She Q1,Q2.
IV.v.51   ta'en] B; tame Q1 (BL); tain Q1 (Fisher, Huntington), Q2,A; taken Q3.
IV.v.86   flay] flea Q1.
V.i.1   VOICES] *om.* Q1
V.i.3   VOICES] *om.* Q1
V.i.32   *Boy*] *om.* Q1,Q2,Q3,A,B.
V.i.53   too] to Q1.
V.i.56   than] then Q1.
V.i.69   o'my] Q2,Q3,A,B; O my Q1.
V.i.71   exchanged] Q2,Q3,A,B; exchange Q1.
V.i.114   than] then Q1.
V.i.178   *gives it to*] Q3,A,B; gives to Q1,Q2.
V.i.206   traitor] Q2,Q3,A,B; taylor Q1.
V.i.254   fever] Q3; favour Q1,Q2,A,B.
V.i.266   will be] Q3; you'l will be Q1; he'll be Q2,A,B. Link amends this phrase to "you'll find will be", following an m.s. note in the Luttrell copy of Q1.

V.i.304	S.D.] Q3; follows Antonio's speech Q1,Q2,A,B.
V.i.335	Antonio] Q3; SP (*Antonio*) Q1,Q2,A.
V.i.365	he is] Q1,Q2,Q3; she is A,B.
V.i.371	for prize] Q3; for prise Q1; my prize Q2,A,B.
V.i.404	you] Q3; *om.* Q1,Q2,A,B.
V.i.413	one] Link,Summers; on Q1,Q2,Q3,A,B.
V.i.423	to] B; too Q1,Q2,Q3,A.
V.i.431	enjoins] A,B; enjoin Q1,Q2,Q3.
V.i.546	*masquers*] Q3,A,B; masqueros Q1,Q2.
Epilogue	
32	gentle] Q3; gentile Q1, Q2; gentle A,B.
39	grimaces] grimasses Q1.

Postscript

	Postscript.] present only in Q1.
22	especially of our sex] this phrase is not present in the first issue of Q1, but is added to some later issues.

Appendix A : Behn on her Work

1. From the "Epistle Dedicatory" to *The Second Part of The Rover*. As it is Acted by the Servants of His Royal Highness. Written by A. Behn. (London: Jacob Tonson, 1681).

[The sequel to *The Rover, or The Banished Cavaliers* is dedicated to James, the Duke of York, younger brother of King Charles II, and later King James II. The passage alludes to the period of Parliamentary rule when James lived in Europe, like his brother Charles and other royalist supporters. As the subtitle, *The Banished Cavaliers*, indicates, Willmore, Belvile, and Frederick are royalists.]

Epistle Dedicatory

"To His Royal Highness the Duke, &c....

This more than human goodness, with the incouragement Your Royal Highness was pleas'd to give the Rover at his first appearance, and the concern you were pleas'd to have for his second, makes me presume to lay him at Your feet; he is a wanderer too, distrest; belov'd, tho unfortunate, and ever constant to Loyalty; were he Legions he should follow and suffer still with so excellent a Prince and Master.... How careless since your glorious Restauration[1] you have been of your Life for the service of your mistaken country the whole world knows, and all brave men admire.

Pardon me then, Great Sir, if I presume to present my faithful soldier, (which no Storms of Fate can ever draw from

---

1 Restauration] The restoration of the monarchy in 1660 followed Oliver Cromwell's death in 1659.

his Obedience) to so great a General and allow him, Royal Sir, a shelter and Protection, who was driven from his Native Country with You, forc'd as you were to fight for his Bread in a strange land, and suffer'd with You all the Ills of Poverty, War, and Banishment, and still Pursues Your Fortunes; and though he cannot serve Your Highness, he may possibly have the Honour of diverting You for a few moments; which tho Your Highness cannot want in a place where all Hearts and Knees are justly bow'd in Adoration, where all conspire, as all the Earth (who have the blessing of Your presence) ought to entertain, serve, and please You; yet this humble Tribute of a most jealous and Devout Heart, may find it amongst your busier hours of greater moment, some one wherein it may have the glory of Your regard, and be capable in some small degree of unbending Your great mind from Royal Cares, the weightiest Cares of all; which if it be so fortunate as to do, I have my end, and the Glory I design, a sufficient reward for her who does and will eternally pray for the Life, Health, and Safety of Your Royal Highness, as in Duty all the World is bound to do, but more especially,

Illustrious Sir,
Your Highnesses most Humble,
most Faithful, and
most Obedient Servant,
A. Behn

2. From "A Pastoral to Mr. Stafford, under the name of Silvio, on his Translation of the Death of Camilla: out of Virgil. By Mrs. Behn. Thirsis and Amarillis" in *Miscellany, or a Collection of Poems by Several Hands. Together with Reflections on Morality or Seneca Unmasqued* (London: 1685): 290-99.

Miscellany, one of three collections of poetry Behn edited in the 1680s, includes poems and poetic translations on a wide variety of topics. "Silvio's" translation of an episode from Virgil's *Aeneid* appeared in *Miscellany Poems Containing a New Translation of Virgil's Eclogues, Ovid's Love Elegies, Odes of Horace and Other Authors, with Several Original poems. By the Most Eminent Hands* (London, 1684), a collection including a preface and poems by John Dryden. (Dryden's translation of *Aeneid* was not published until 1696.) Behn's "A Pastoral to Mr. Stafford" commends "Silvio's" representation of Camilla,* a heroic woman warrior whom Behn describes thus in the poem:

> Never was fighting in our *Sex* a Charm,
> Till *Silvio* did the bright *Camilla* Arm;
> With Noble Modesty he shews us how
> To be at once *Hero* and *Woman* too.(297)

Earlier in the same poem, in one of the few references Behn makes in her works to her own history, Behn refers to her intelligence work for the government of King Charles II in Antwerp in 1666:

> Once *Thirsis*, by th' *Arcadian* King's Commands,
> I left these Shades, to visit forein [sic] Lands;
> Imploy'd in public toiles of State Affairs,
> Unusual with my Sex, or to my Years.(295)

*Camilla's heroic actions in battle and her ultimate death are recounted in the eleventh book of Virgil's *Aeneid*.

Appendix B: From Early Accounts of Behn's Life

1. From *Female Poems on Several Occasions. Written by Ephelia*. (London, 1679): 72-3.

[In this poem "Ephelia" uses a contemporary variant spelling of Behn's name. The identity of "Ephelia" is not known. Recently, in her facsimile edition of *Female Poems on Several Occasions*, Maureen A. Mulvihill suggested that "Ephelia" is Joan Philips, a pseudonym for Anne Prowde of Shrewesbury. See Mulvihill's edition, *Poems by Ephelia (c. 1679): The Premier Facsimile Edition* (Delmar, New York: Scholar's Facsimiles and Reprints, 1992: 65-77.)]

To Madam Bhen

Madam! permit a Muse, that has been long
Silent with wonder, now to find a Tongue:
Forgive that Zeal I can no longer hide,
And pardon a necessitated Pride.
When first your strenuous polite Lines I read,
At once it Wonder and Amazement bred,
To see such things flow from a Womans Pen,
As might be Envy'd by the wittiest Men:
You write so sweetly, that at once you move,
The Ladies Jealousies, and Gallant's Love;
Passions so gentle, and so well exprest,
As needs must be the same fill your own Breast;
Then Rough again, as your Inchanting Quill
Commanded Love, or Anger at your Will:
As in your Self, so in your Verses meet,
A rare connexion of Strong and Sweet:
This I admir'd at, and my Pride to show,
Have took the Vanity to tell you so

In humble Verse, that has the Luck to please
Some Rustick Swains, or silly Shepherdess:
But far unfit to reach your Sacred Ears,
Or stand your Judgment: Oh! my conscious Fears
Check my Presumption, yet I must go on,
And finish the rash Task I have begun.
Condemn it Madam, if you please, to th'Fire,
It gladly will your Sacrifice expire,
As sent by one, that rather chose to shew
Her want of Skill, than want of Zeal to you.

**2. From Gerard Langbaine, *An Account of the English
Dramatick Poets. Or, Some Observations and Remarks on the
Lives and Writings, of all those that have Publish'd either
Comedies, Tragedies, Tragi-Comedies, Pastorals, Masques,
Interludes, Farces, or Operas in the English Tongue.* 2 vols.
(Oxford, 1691).**

[Langbaine's valuable work assembles information about a
great many plays of the period from 1660-1690. One of Langbaine's main interests was to document the plays by early seventeenth-century writers such as Shakespeare, Fletcher, and
Jonson which had been adapted by Restoration playwrights.
In the "Preface," Langbaine says he wants to vindicate the
early playwrights by "exposing our Modern Plagiaries" (1:a4).
See discussions of charges against Behn of plagiarism in the
"Introduction" (13,15,21-2).]

Mrs. Astraea Behn

A Person lately deceased, but whose Memory will be long
fresh amongst the Lovers of Dramatick Poetry, as having
been sufficiently Eminent not only for her Theatrical Performances, but several other Pieces both in Verse and Prose;
which gain'd her an Esteem among the Wits, almost equal to
that of the incomparable *Orinda*, Madame *Katharine Phillips*
(of whom we shall speak hereafter). Her Plays are Sixteen in
number, having therein exceeded any of the Poets of this
Age, Sr. *William Davenant*, and Mr. *Dryden*, excepted. Most of

her Comedies have had the good fortune to please: and tho'
it must be confest that she has borrow'd very much, not only
from her own Country Men, but likewise from the French Poets: yet it may be said in her behalf, that she has often been
forc'd to it through hast: and has borrow'd from others
Stores rather of Choice than for want of a fond[1] of Wit of her
own: it having been formerly her unhappiness to be necessitated to write for Bread, as she has publisht to the world.[2]
'Tis also to her Commendation, that whatever she borrows
she improves for the better: a Plea which our late Laureat has
not been asham'd to make use of.[3] If to this, her *Sex* may
plead in her behalf, I doubt not that she will be allowed equal
with several of our Poets her Contemporaries. I shall now
give an Account of her Plays in an Alphabetical Order, as follows: (1.17-18)

. . . .

Rover, or *The Banisht Cavaleers*, in Two parts, both of them
Comedies, Acted at the Duke's Theatre, and printed in
quarto, *Lond.* 1677, and 1681, the Second Part being Dedicated to his Royal Highness the Duke. These are the only
Comedies, for the Theft of which, I condemn this ingenious
Authoress; they being so excellent in their Original, that 'tis
pity they should have been alter'd: and notwithstanding her
Apology in the Postscript to the first part; I cannot acquit her
of prevarication, since *Angelica* is not *the only stol'n Object*, as
she calls it: she having borrow'd largely throughout. The
truth is, the better to disguise her Theft, she has (as the in-

---

1   fond] fund

2   Pref. to *Patient Fancy* (Langbaine's note)] Behn's play was first performed in
     1688. She says that she "is forced to write for Bread and not ashamed to owne
     it." ("To the Reader", *Sir Patient Fancy* in *The Works of Aphra Behn*, ed. Janet
     Todd (Columbus: Ohio State University Press, 1996): 3.5.

3   Pref. to *Mock Astrologer* (Langbaine's note)] John Dryden's play, *An Evening's
     Love, or the Mock Astrologer*, was first produced in 1668 and printed in 1671. In
     the "Preface" Dryden defends dramatic adaptation of the plots of earlier plays
     or stories (*The Works of John Dryden* (Berkeley, Los Angeles, London: University
     of California Press, 1970): 10.210-13). Dryden was Poet Laureate from 1670-89.

genious *Scarron* observes of the Writers of Romances,)[4] *Flea'd*[5] *the Eel by beginning at the Tail*; yet notwithstanding, what she has omitted of worth in her first part, she has taken into the second; and therefore could not justly call these Plays her own.

3. From "The History of the Life and Memoirs of Mrs. Behn. Written by One of the Fair Sex" in *All the Histories and Novels Written by the Late Ingenious Mrs. Behn. 2 vols. 8th ed. (London, 1735) 1: 1-73.

["The History of the Life and Memoirs of Mrs. Behn", first published by Charles Gildon in the third edition of *All the Histories and Novels* (1698), is the first account of Behn's life. See "Introduction" (10-13) for a discussion of this early biography, which sets the pattern for many later biographies by treating statements by Behn's narrators biographically.]

"The History of the Life and Memoirs of Mrs. Behn. Written by One of the Fair Sex"

My intimate Acquaintance with the admirable *Astrea*, gave me naturally a very great Esteem for her; for it both freed me from that Folly of my Sex, of envying or slighting Excellencies, I could not obtain, and inspired me with a noble Fire to celebrate that Woman, who was an Honour and Glory to our Sex: and this reprinting her incomparable Novels, presented me with a lucky Occasion of exerting that Desire into Action.

She was a Gentlewoman by Birth, of a good Family in the City of *Canterbury* in *Kent*; her Father's Name was *Johnson*, whose Relation to the Lord *Willoughby*, drew him, for the advantageous Post of Lieutenant-General of many Isles, besides the Continent of *Surinam*, from his quiet Retreat at *Canter-*

---

4   City Romance, *pag* 2. (Langbaine's note)] Paul Scarron (1610-60) was a prolific
     French comic writer.
5   Flea'd] flayed

bury, to run the hazardous Voyage of the *West-Indies*. With him he took his chief Riches, his Wife and Children; and in that Number *Afra*, his promising Darling, our future *Heroine*, and admired *Astrea*, who even in the first Bud of Infancy, discovered such early Hopes of her riper Years, that she was equally her Parents Joy and Fears: for they too often mistrust the Loss of a Child, whose Wit and Understanding outstrip its Years, as too great a Blessing to be long enjoy'd. Whether that Fear proceeds from Superstition or Diffidence of our present Happiness, I shall not determine; but must pursue my Discourse, with assuring you, none had greater Fears of that Nature, or greater Cause for 'em: for besides the Vivacity and Wit of her Conversation at the first Use almost of Reason in Discourse, she would write the prettiest, soft, engaging Verses in the World. Thus qualified, she accompany'd her Parents in their long Voyage to *Surinam*, leaving behind her the Sighs and Tears of all her Friends, and breaking Hearts of her Lovers, that sighed to possess what was scarce yet arrived to a Capacity of easing their Pain, if she had been willing. But as she was Mistress of uncommon Charms of Body as well as Mind, she gave infinite and raging Desires, before she could know the least herself.

Her Father liv'd not to see that Land flowing with Milk and Honey, that Paradise which she so admirably describes in *Oroonoko*:[6] where you may also find what Adventures happen'd to her in that Country. The Misfortunes of that Prince had been unknown to us, if the divine *Astrea* had not been there, and his Sufferings had wanted that Satisfaction which her Pen has given 'em in the Immortality of his Virtues and Constancy; the very Memory of which moves a generous Pity in all, and a Contempt of the brutal Actors in that unfortunate Tragedy. Here I can add nothing to what she has given the World already, but a Vindication of her from some unjust Aspersions I find are insinuated about this Town in Relation to that Prince. I knew her intimately well, and I believe she

---

6   *Oroonoko*] see "Introduction" (12-13) for a discussion of Behn's time in Surinam and the composition of *Oroonoko*.

would not have concealed any Love-Affair from me, being one of her own Sex, whose Friendship and Secrecy she had experienced: which makes me assure the World there was no Affair between that Prince and *Astrea*, but what the whole Plantation were Witnesses of; a generous Value for his uncommon Virtues, which every one that but hears 'em, finds in himself, and his Presence gave her no more. Besides his Heart was too violently set on the everlasting Charms of his *Imoinda*, to be shook with those more faint (in his Eye) of a White Beauty; and *Astrea's* Relations, there present, had too watchful an Eye over her, to permit the Frailty of her Youth, if that had been powerful enough. As this is false, so are the Consequences of it too; for the Lord, her Father's Friend, that was not then arrived, perished in a Hurricane, without having it in his Power to resent it: Nor had his Resentments been any thing to her, who only waited the Arrival of the next Ships to convey her back to her desired *England*; where she soon after, to her Satisfaction, arrived, and gave King *Charles* II so pleasant and rational an Account of his Affairs there, and particularly of the Misfortunes of *Oroonoko*, that he desired her to deliver them publickly to the World, and was satisfy'd of her Abilities in the Management of Business, and the Fidelity of our *Heroine* to his Interest. After she was marry'd to Mr. *Behn*, a Merchant of this City, tho' of *Dutch* Extraction, he committed to her Secrecy and Conduct, Affairs of the highest Importance in the *Dutch* War; which obliging her to stay at *Antwerp*, presented her with the Adventures of Prince *Tarquin*, and his false wicked Fair-One *Miranda*.[7]

The full Account of which you will find admirably writ in the following Collection.

But I must not omit entirely some other Adventures that happened to her during this Negotiation; tho' I cannot give so just and large a Representation of them as I willingly would.

---

7   *Tarquin* and *Miranda*] Behn's prose romance *The Fair Jilt*, first published in 1688.

I have told you, that as her Mind, so her Body was adorned with all the Advantages of our Sex: Wit, Beauty, and Judgment seldom meet in one, especially in Woman, (you may allow this from a Woman) but in her they were eminent: and this made her turn all the Advantages each gave her, to the Interest she had devoted herself to serve. And whereas the Beauty of the Face is that which generally takes with Mankind, so it gives 'em most commonly an Assurance and Security from Designs; for they suppose that a beautiful Woman, as she is made for the Pleasure of others, so chiefly minds her own: and in that they are not much mistaken, for they pursue the same Course with the rest of the World, Pleasure; but then 'tis as various as their Tempers, and what they generally imagine may have the least Share in many of them. The Event, I'm sure, shew'd that in *Astrea* (at this Time at least) the Pleasures of Love had not the Predominance, when she diverted the Hopes, which the Vanity of a *Dutch* Merchant of great Interest and Authority in *Holland*, had entertained of a successful Passion, to the Service of her Prince, and his own shameful Disappointment. (1-6)

. . . .

Here I must draw to an End: for tho' considerable Trusts were repos'd in her, yet they were of that Import, that I must not presume here to insert 'em; but shall conclude with her Death, occasion'd by an unskilful Physician, on the 16th of *April*, 1689. She was buried in the Cloysters of *Westminster-Abby*, cover'd only with a plain Marble Stone, with two wretched Verses on it, made, as I'm inform'd by a very ingenious Gentleman, tho' no Poet: the very Person, whom the Envious of our Sex, and the Malicious of the other, would needs have the Author of most of her's; which, to my knowledge, were her own Product, without the Assistance of any Thing but Nature, which shews itself indeed without the Embarassments of Art in every Thing she has wrote.

She was of a generous and open Temper, something passionate, very serviceable to her Friends in all that was in her Power; and could sooner forgive an Injury, than do one. She had Wit, Honour, Good-humour, and Judgment. She was

Mistress of all the pleasing Arts of Conversation, but us'd 'em not to any but those who love Plain-dealing. She was a Woman of Sense, and by Consequence a Lover of Pleasure, as indeed all, both Men and Women, are; but only some would be thought to be above the Conditions of Humanity, and place their chief Pleasure in a proud vain Hypocrisy. For my Part, I knew her intimately, and never saw aught unbecoming the just Modesty of our Sex, tho' more gay and free than the Folly of the Precise will allow. She was, I'm satisfy'd, a greater Honour to our Sex, than all the Canting Tribe of Dissemblers, that die with the false Reputation of Saints. This I may venture to say, because I'm unknown, and the revengeful Censures of my Sex will not reach me, since they will never to able to draw the Veil, and discover the Speaker of these bold Truths. If I have done my dead Friend any Manner of Justice, I'm satisfy'd, having obtain'd my End: If not, the Reader must remember that there are few *Astrea's* arise in our Age, and 'till such a one does appear, all our Endeavours in Encomiums on the last must be vain and impotent (72-3).

4. From *The Poetical Register or, the Lives and Characters of the English Dramatick Poets. With an Account of their Writings*. (London: E. Curll, 1719):14-17.

[Curll's comments on *The Rover* are based on Langbaine's account.]

Mrs. Afra Behn.

Mrs. Behn was born in the City of *Canterbury*; her Maiden Name *Johnson*; and she was no less admir'd in her Youth for her Beauty,
    than in her riper Years for Poetical Performances, in which she excell'd all of her own Sex in the Age she liv'd, and exceeded many of her Contemporary Poets of the other. She had a Facility in Writing; most of her Comedies had the good Fortune to please; and tho' she borrow'd very much from the *French* Poets, and her own Countrymen, yet it proceeded rather from Haste, than want of a sprightly Wit of her own.

She had a strong Natural Genius, which shew'd itself in every Thing she writ; and she was not only eminent for her Theatrical Performances, but also for several other Pieces, both in Verse and Prose. Her Plays are Seventeen in Number. (14)

. . . .

VI. *The Rover*, or *The Banish'd Cavaliers*, in Two Parts, both Comedies, Acted at the Duke of *York's* Theatre, in the Years 1677, and 1681. The Second Part Dedicated to his Royal Highness the Duke. These Plays have a great deal of Wit in them; but they are mostly taken from *Killigrew's Don Thomaso*, or *The Wanderer*. (15)

. . . .

Mrs. Behn Died in the Year 1689, and lies interr'd in the Cloyster of *Westminster-Abby*, under a Black Marble Stone, with this Inscription;

Here lies a Proof that WIT *can never be*
Defence enough against MORTALITY. (17)

5. From *A General Dictionary, Historical and Critical: In Which A New and Accurate Translation of that of the Celebrated Mr. Bayle, with the Corrections and Observations printed in the Late Edition at Paris is included; and interspersed with several thousand Lives never before published. The Whole containing the History of the Most Illustrious Persons of all Ages and Nations, particularly those of Great Britain and Ireland, distinguished by their Rank, Actions, Learning and other Accomplishments. With Reflections on such Passages of Mr. Bayle, as seem to favour Scepticism and the Manichee System. By the Reverend Mr. John Peter Bernard; The Reverend Mr. Thomas Birch, M.A. and F.R.S., Mr. John Lockman; and other Hands, 10 vols.* (**London, 1734-41**): **3.140-49.**

[The long essay on Behn which is excerpted here is one of the entries added to the English translation of Pierre Bayle's dictionary. The article on Behn includes many detailed notes and glosses; only the last note is included here.]

BEHN (APHARA), was descended from a good family in the city of Canterbury in Kent, and her maiden name was Johnson. I have not been able to find the date of her birth. She past her childhood in the abovementioned city, where she gave the most promising hopes, of her excelling one day in the perfections both of mind and body. She discovered a strong inclination for Poetry from her early years, at which time she would write verses inimitably soft and pretty. She was very young when she went with her father and the rest of her family to Surinam, in the West-Indies, which voyage was in nothing so considerable, as its giving rise to the tender History of Oroonoko, (whence the idea of the celebrated Tragedy so intitled was taken) which the Author of Mrs. Behn's Life assures us, was written by the express command of King Charles the Second, to whom she was introduced, on which occasion she gave his Majesty a pleasing and just account of the state of the Colony abovementioned. The disappointment she met with in her fortune, by losing her parents and relations in that country, obliged her to return to England; and coming to London, she was afterwards married to

Mr. Behn, an eminent Merchant of that City, but of Dutch extraction. She now had gained so great a reputation for wit as well as judgment; and, what is still more uncommon in her sex, for secrecy, that she was employed by King Charles the Second, in the time of the Dutch war, in several negotiations in Flanders, which required industry and caution; and in those she acquitted herself with all the applause that success could entitle an ingenious beautiful woman to, from a Monarch who had so great a value for the fair sex. It is related that Mrs. Behn, by her intrigues, discovered a secret of the highest importance to the British Nation, which she communicated to a certain Minister; but he slighting the intelligence, she laid aside political affairs, and devoted her self, during the rest of her stay in Antwerp, to pleasure. She her self takes notice, in one of her Poems, of her being employed by the King in an affair of State.[8] Whether that Monarch was grateful to her is not known, but the softness of his Court gave her a more immediate occasion of exerting her poetical genius, by which she diverted the gay part of the town for several years. She seems to have been personally acquainted with the greatest wits of her time, some of whom have honoured her with encomiums, as Mr. Dryden, Mr. Southerne, Mr. Charles Cotton and others. Mr. Gildon,[9] who was familiarly acquainted with her, speaks of her with enthusiasm, calling her the incomparable Mrs. Behn, and saying, that the reflection on the unhappy circumstances in which she wrote, ought to raise our admiration of her, whose genius was of that force, like Homer's, to maintain its gaiety, in the midst of disappointments. To draw her to the life, says the same Author in another place, one must write like her, that is with all the softness of her sex, and all the fire of ours. But great deductions ought often to be made from the applauses of a Writer

---

8   Affair of state] See Behn's comment on this period of her life in the extract
     from her poem in Appendix A, p.199.
9   Mr. Gildon] Charles Gildon published the collection of Behn's work preceded
     by the biographical account by "One of the Fair Sex," part of which is included
     in Appendix B, 3. Some of the details about Behn here attributed to Gildon are
     not included in the account by "One of the Fair Sex."

of our sex, when bestowed on a beautiful woman of genius, with whom he is intimate. Besides, Mr. Gildon's judgement will hardly pass for current with persons of a good taste. The same Writer informs us, that she was vastly witty in conversation, and reasoned with much more judgement than is usually found in persons of her sex. That she would argue, on the nicest metaphysical points, with the utmost strength, and the most happy distinctions: would enforce, very engagingly, her notions, with all the justness of the most able Philosopher, though not with his majestic (I suppose he means *majesterial*) roughness; which made all she said more prevalent with her hearers. That she could talk on all subjects, and was never impertinent: that her wit was not sullied by vanity; she never discovering her merit any otherwise than by the fine things she spoke, which obliged others to bestow so much applause on her, that she was never reduced to the awkward necessity of praising her self: that her Muse was never subject to the curse of bringing forth with pain, but that she always writ with the greatest ease, and that too in the midst of company, and discourse of other matters. Mr. Gildon informs us at the same time, that he himself saw her write part of Oroonoko, and discourse in her turn with the persons then in the room. (3.140-43)

. . . .

Whether or no she was woman of strict virtue, I shall not take upon me to determine, but it is certain her Comedies cannot very well boast that character; and if the chief requisite in a dramatic performance be moral instruction, Mrs. Behn's cannot merit any elogium on that account. The passions, that of love especially (says a Writer) she was mistress of, and gave us such nice, such tender touches of them, that without her name we might discover the Author, as Protogenes did Apelles[10] by the stroke of his pencil. That she was of a very

---

10   Protogenes and Apelles] Protogenes was a Greek painter and sculptor of the
      fourth century B.C.; Apelles was a painter during the same period.

tender and amorous cast appears from all her composi-
tions.... (3.145)

. . . .

Though Mrs. Behn borrowed so largely from other Writers, it
is nevertheless certain that she was mistress of a great fund of
invention. She seems, as I observed, to have writ in too great
a hurry, to give the requisite correctness and delicacy to her
diction, and this is much more apparent, (as it naturally
must) in her poetical productions. For though a poet be inspired with ever so great a genius, yet the expressing of his
ideas in strong, beautiful verse will generally cost him no little pains. There are indeed some happy moments, in which
the brightest expressions will pour upon his imagination; but
these do not come every day. All who are born with a genius
know by experience, that there is the critical minute (l'heure
du Berger)[11] no less in writing of Poetry than in Love. This
must be snatched as it flies, and the best use possible made of
it; for it is then that the greatest Poet surpasses himself. After
this Article was gone to press, I had an opportunity of seeing
Mr. Bowman,[12] one of his Majesty's Company of Comedians,
belonging to the Theatre Royal in Drury-Lane, who informed
me of some particulars relating to our Poetess.*

   * [*Some particulars relating to our Poetess*] I am very much
obliged to this Gentleman, for the readiness and civility with
which he offered to assist me in this; or any other occasion in
his power relating to the Theatre. Mr. Bowman was well acquainted with Mrs. Behn, who, he informs me, was very
agreeable in her person, had fine eyes, and was of a very

---

11   l'heure du Berger] literally, "the shepherd's hour"; figuratively, a moment
    favourable for lovers.

12   Mr. Bowman] John Boman or Bowman (1651?-1739), an actor and singer
    associated with Dorset Garden Theatre in the period when Behn's plays were
    produced there. He played Frederick in *The Rover* at Drury Lane Theatre in
    1710, and was still acting in the 1730s. See *A Biographical Dictionary of Actors,
    Actresses, Musicians, Dancers, Managers and Other Stage Personnel in London,
    1660-1800*, (2.198-202).

graceful stature. He confirmed the truth of what is related by her Life-writers, *viz.* of the uncommon sprightliness of her conversation. He also had known some instances of the great facility of her pen, by the swiftness with which she writ some dramatic pieces, in which he himself performed. He told me one circumstance relating to Mrs. Barry, who was so long the ornament of the English stage, viz. that Mrs. Behn, upon her writing of *The Rover, or Banisht Cavalier,* took the utmost pains to instruct that Actress, who was to play the part of Helena in that Comedy; and that the beauty of Mrs. Barry's action on this Occasion, proved the foundation of the great fame she afterwards gained.

Her taste of life was perfectly Anacreontic.[13] She was always for enjoying the present moment.... Mr. Bowman believes that Mrs. Behn was about fifty when she died; if so, she was born about the year 1639, or 1640, in the reign of Charles I. (3:148-9).

---

13   Anacreontic] Anacreon, who flourished about 570 B.C., was a Greek lyric poet whose subject matter was frequently pleasure.

Appendix C: Adaptation

From *Love in Many Masks as Altered by J.P. Kemble from Mrs. Behn's Rover* (London: [1790]):69-73.

[The first performance of John Philip Kemble's adaptation of *The Rover* took place on March 8, 1790 at the Theatre Royal in Drury Lane with Kemble as Willmore. Dorah Jordan, a popular comic performer, played Helena (as Kemble spells the name). The adaptation is briefly discussed in the "Introduction" (35).

This passage from *Love in Many Masks* adapts *The Rover* V.i.385-553.]

Exit Belville and Pedro. Willmore is following them. Enter Helena, as before, in Boys Clothes.

HELENA.

Tack about, tack about, Neptune — whither bound?

WILLMORE.

Into the harbour of thy arms, thy fair Amphitrite — Now, a thousand blessings on thee for this kindness; egad, child, I was e'en in despair of ever seeing thee again; my friends are all provided for within, each man his kind woman.

HELENA.

Hah! I thought they had serv'd me some such trick!

WILLMORE.

And I was e'en resolv'd to go aboard, and condemn myself to my lone cabin, and thoughts of thee.

HELENA.

And cou'd you have left me behind; wou'd you have been so ill natur'd?

WILLMORE.

Why, 'twould have broke my heart, child — but since we are met again, I defy foul weather to part us. Therefore, dear creature, since we are so well agreed, let's lose no time, but run away to my lodgings? — Come — I love to steal a bird and a bottle with a friend, and hate long graces — come, come. —

HELENA.

'Tis but getting my consent, and the bus'ness is soon done; let but Hymen and his priest say amen to't — and you may take me as soon as you will, my good Captain Love-in-a-hurry.

WILLMORE.

Hold, hold, no bugg words, child; priest and Hymen! Prithee, add hang-man to make up the concert, — no, no, we'll have no vows but love, child, nor witness but the lovers: Hymen and priest wait still upon portion and join-ture; love and beauty have their own ceremonies. Mar-riage is as certain a bane to love, as lending money is to friendship: I'll neither ask nor give a vow — though I could be content to turn gipsy, and become a left-handed bridegroom, to have the pleasure of working that great miracle of making a maid a mother, if you durst venture; 'tis upsy gipsy that, and, if I miss, I lose my labour.

HELENA.

And if you do not lose, what shall I get? A cradle full of noise and mischief, with a pack of shame and repentance at my back! 'Tis upsy gipsy that, and I lose my labour.

WILLMORE.

Well, I have tried you too far, and ask pardon for my seeming rudeness — I see there's no way to conquer good-nature, but by yielding — One kiss, and I am thine.

HELENA.

One kiss! How like my page he speaks. I am resolved you shall have none, for asking such a sneaking sum. He that will be satisfied with one kiss, will never die of that long-ing. Good friend Single-kiss, is all your talking come to this? — A kiss, a caudle! Farewel, Captain — Single-kiss.

Going out, he stops her.

WILLMORE.

Nay, by Heaven, both the Indies shall not buy thee from me. I adore thy humour, and will marry thee: and we are so of one humour, it must be a bargain — Give me thy hand. [*Kisses her hand.*] And now let the blind ones, Love and Fortune, do their worst.

HELENA.

Why, Gad-a-mercy, Captain!

WILLMORE.

But hark'ye — the bargain is now made; but is it not fit we should know each other's names? that when we have reason to curse one another hereafter, and people ask me who 'tis I give to the devil, I may at least be able to tell what family you came of.

HELENA.

Good reason, Captain: and where I have cause, as I doubt not but I shall have, that I may know at whom to throw my — blessings, I beseech ye your name.

WILLMORE.

I am called Robert the Constant.

HELENA.

A very fine name. Pray, was it your falconer or butler that christen'd you? Do they not use to whistle when they call you?

WILLMORE.

I hope you have a better, that a man may name without crossing himself, you are so merry with mine.

HELENA.

I am called Helena the Inconstant.

Enter Pedro, Belville, Florinda, Frederick, Valeria.

PEDRO.

Ha! Helena!

FLORINDA.

Helena!

HELENA.

The very same — Ha! my brother! — Now, Captain, shew your love and courage; stand to your arms, and defend me bravely, or I am lost for ever.

PEDRO.

What's this I hear! False girl, how came you hither, and what's your business? Speak.

WILLMORE.

Hold off, Sir; you have leave to parly only.

HELENA.

I had e'en as good tell it, as you guess it. Faith, brother, my business is the same with all living creatures of my age — to love, and be beloved — and here's the man.

PEDRO.

Perfidious maid! Hast thou deceived me too, deceived thyself, and Heaven?

HELENA.

'Tis time enough to make my peace with that.
Be you but kind, let me alone with Heaven.

PEDRO.

Belville, I did not expect this false play from you. Was't not enough you gain'd Florinda, which I pardoned, but your libertine friends too must be enriched with the spoils of a noble family?

BELVILLE.

Faith, Sir, I am as much surprised at this as you can be: yet, Sir, my friend's a gentleman, and ought to be esteemed for his profession. His bravery has been often proved in bloody battles for his country's rights; he has the honour to serve the best of men and Kings; and, though a private man, yet every Captain in the British navy is himself a King aboard his little wooden world.

PEDRO.

What's this to the maintenance of a woman of her birth and fortune?

WILLMORE.

Faith, Sir, I can boast of nothing but a sword, which does me right where'er I come, and has defended a worse cause than a woman's; and since I really loved her before I either knew her birth or fortune, I must pursue my resolution still, and marry her.

PEDRO.

And is all your holy intent of becoming a nun changed to this at last?

HELENA.

Why, I have considered the matter, brother, and find the two hundred thousand crowns my uncle left me will be better laid out on love than a nunnery, and turn to as good an account — Let most voices carry it — for the nunnery, or the Captain?

ALL CRY,

A Captain! a Captain!

HELENA.

There, there; — they are all for the Captain.

PEDRO.

Come — there's one motive induces me — take her — I shall now be free from fears of her honour; guard it you now, if you can — I have been a slave to't long enough.

WILLMORE.

Sir, I am of a nation that are of opinion a woman's honour is not worth guarding, when she has a mind to part with it.

HELENA.

Well said, Captain.

PEDRO.

This was your plot, mistress; but I hope you have married one that will revenge my quarrel to you.

To Valeria.

VALERIA.

There's no altering destiny, Sir.

PEDRO.

Sooner than a woman's will; therefore I forgive you all, and wish you may get my father's pardon as easily. Who comes here?

Enter Blunt, dressed in a Spanish habit, looking very ridiculously; followed by a Taylor.

TAYLOR.

'Tis very well, Sir —

BLUNT.

Well, Sir! 'dsheartlikins, I tell you 'tis damnable ill, Sir — A Spanish habit! — Could the devil and my taylor devise no other punishment for me, but the mode of a nation I abominate?

Exit Taylor.

BELVILLE.

What's the matter, Ned?

BLUNT.

Pray view me round, and judge.

Turns round.

BELVILLE.

I must confess thou art a kind of an odd figure.

BLUNT.

In a Spanish habit with a vengeance! A pillory were an easy collar to this. In fine, Gentlemen, methinks I look altogether like a bag of baize stuffed full of fool's flesh.

BELVILLE.

Methinks 'tis well, and makes thee look *en cavalier.* — Come, Sir, settle your face, and salute our friend's Lady —

BLUNT.

> Ha! — say'st thou so? [*To Helena.*] Lady — (if you be one), give me leave to kiss your hand, and tell you, adsheartlikins, for all I look so, I am your humble servant. — A plague of this Spanish habit!

WILLMORE.

> Come, we'll to the good man within, who waits to give us a cast of his office. Don't you tremble at the thought of giving yourself to a fellow of so wild a character?

HELENA.

> No more than you do in a battle or a storm.

WILLMORE.

> Thou'rt a brave girl! — I admire thy love and courage, and will give thee as little cause as I can to repent 'em.
> Henceforth no other pleasures can I know,
> Than those of fond fidelity to you;
> Your pow'r my captive heart in chains shall bind,
> Sweet as the graces of your face and mind: —
> Blest in my friends, and doubly blest in love,
> My joy's complete indeed — if you approve.

Exeunt.

THE END.

LIST
of products used:

896 lb(s) of Rolland Enviro100 Print
100% post-consumer

RESULTS
Based on the Cascades products you selected
compared to products in the industry made with
100% virgin fiber, your savings are:

 8 trees

 7,413 gal. US of water
80 days of water consumption

 937 lbs of waste
9 waste containers

 2,436 lbs CO_2
4,619 miles driven

 12 MMBTU
57,768 60W light bulbs for one hour

 7 lbs NOx
emissions of one truck during 10
days